M.I. Franklin
Change the Record – Punk Women Music Politics

Culture & Theory

For Zeena

M.I. Franklin (PhD) is full professor and chair of media, cultural industries and society at the University of Groningen.

M.I. Franklin
Change the Record — Punk Women Music Politics

[transcript]

Bibliographic information published by the Deutsche Nationalbibliothek
The Deutsche Nationalbibliothek lists this publication in the Deutsche Nationalbibliografie; detailed bibliographic data are available in the Internet at https://dnb.dnb.de

© 2024 transcript Verlag, Bielefeld

All rights reserved. No part of this book may be reprinted or reproduced or utilized in any form or by any electronic, mechanical, or other means, now known or hereafter invented, including photocopying and recording, or in any information storage or retrieval system, without permission in writing from the publisher.

Cover layout: Maria Arndt, Bielefeld
Typeset: Gerbach, Bielefeld
Printed by Majuskel Medienproduktion GmbH, Wetzlar
Print-ISBN 978-3-8376-4171-4
PDF-ISBN 978-3-8394-4171-8
https://doi.org/10.14361/9783839441718
ISSN of series: 2702-8968
eISSN of series: 2702-8976

Printed on permanent acid-free text paper.

Table of Contents

LIST OF FIGURES 7

ACKNOWLEDGEMENTS 9

1. INTRO 11
To the Front 11
Beyond Fanstalgia 13
What Makes Punk Music (Not)? 18
Reader Notes 22
Which Books and Why 23
Chapter Outline 27
Setting Out 28

2. MUSICIANS AS MEMOIRISTS 29
Punk Performance Sexual Politics 29
Punk Public Archives 33
The Memoirs: 'Dear Reader' 44
Outro: Punk as Art 50

3. FINDING VOICE 51
Intro 51
Into the *Voice* 52
Punking up the Pop Rock Canon 56
Rebel Rebel 67

4. GRRRLS WITH GUITARS 71
Intro 71
Guitars Guitars Guitars 74
Bodies Bodies Bodies: Woman with Guitar 77
Punk Musica Practica 88
Outro 90

5. VANGUARD OR OLD GUARD? 95
Hip Priestess: Coat, Skirt, Hair, Hat 95
'Punk and Poses' 99
Race-Gender-Class Horizons 104
Since – On Getting Younger 110
Nina Simone – She Who Did It First 119

6. OUTRO 123
Sex, Gender and Public Culture 123
How Did We Get Here? 124
Listening to Music Writing 126
Punk and Current Events 127
Fade Up 133

APPENDIX: THE MEMOIR-SET 135

BIBLIOGRAPHY 137

NOTES 145

LIST OF FIGURES

Figure 1:	Carrie Brownstein, Artist: Mauricio Escobar	13
Figure 2:	Brix Smith Start, Artist: Mauricio Escobar	21
Figure 3:	Diptych – Cosey Fanni Tutti and Viv Albertine, Artist: Mauricio Escobar	26
Figure 4:	Nina Hagen, Artist: Mauricio Escobar	37
Figure 5:	Diptych – Alice Bag, Artist: Mauricio Escobar	44
Figure 6:	Diptych – Kim Gordon and Patti Smith, Artist: Mauricio Escobar	58
Figure 7:	Diptych – Patti Smith, Artist: Mauricio Escobar	61
Figure 8:	Nina Hagen, Artist: Mauricio Escobar	64
Figure 9:	Brix Smith Start (reprise), Artist: Mauricio Escobar	66
Figure 10:	Cosey Fanni Tutti, Artist: Mauricio Escobar	73
Figure 11:	Viv Albertine (and guitar), Artist: Mauricio Escobar	80
Figure 12:	Diptych – Carrie Brownstein and Kim Gordon, Artist: Mauricio Escobar	85
Figure 13:	Diptych – Kim Gordon and Brix Smith Start, Artist: Mauricio Escobar	89
Figure 14:	Patti Smith, Artist: Mauricio Escobar	98
Figure 15:	Pauline Black (with hat), Artist: Mauricio Escobar	102
Figure 16:	Chrissie Hynde, Artist: Mauricio Escobar	107
Figure 17:	Pauline Black, Artist: Mauricio Escobar	111
Figure 18:	Diptych – Chrissie Hynde and Nina Hagen, Artist: Mauricio Escobar	116
Figure 19:	Nina Simone (at the piano), Artist: Mauricio Escobar	120
Figure 20:	Kim Gordon, Artist: Mauricio Escobar	129
Figure 21:	Nina Simone, Artist: Mauricio Escobar	132

ACKNOWLEDGEMENTS

Work on this study began back in 2017 as a (rather long) conference paper. I uploaded the paper onto a 'free' online academic publishing platform, convinced that the book version would be completed in punk-like fashion, quickly. It was not. Other projects and events, the Covid-19 pandemic not included, intervened. What the hell. Here I am, six years – a lifetime – later with the book-length version of that paper in print*. There are people to thank for their support and faith in this labour of love, by someone who was not-strictly-punk but who revelled in that generation's refusal to be groomed and tuned by the global music industrial complex. Great role models then, and now even if I don't have all their records, haven't seen all of them performing live, or agree with everything they say. Two people have made formative contributions to the book that is in front of you: Jakob Horstmann from transcipt press signed me up back when, accepted the many delays and read draft chapters one by one with an open mind and a sharp eye: an editor we dream about as scholars with interests and passions that bump against the tarnished ivory towers in which we work. Mauricio Escobar whose portraits of the musician-memoirists explored here provided me with another eye and a visual artist's sensibility, and creative energy. We had fun putting the artwork together, a precious gift from the artist, and for which I am very grateful. Others have sustained me as friends, confidants, and all-round fabulous people in my life during the work for this project, and all that other stuff. Thank you, thank you, thank you to: Lesley, Henri, and Cat Astier, Katie, Peter, and Paul Beyer, Valentina Cardo, Elizabeth Coombs, Zeena Feldman, Pierre Florac, Angela Franklin, Thomas Gaugenot, Jim Huntington and Nicky Harrison, Minda Moreira, Mary Newman, David Reynolds, Gareth Stanton, Pollyanna Stokoe, Helen Taber, Katrina Taylor, Margaret Tibbles, and Derek Unwin.

*The paper – "Rock-Chic(k) Lit: Vanguard or Old Guard?" – was presented on Panel WA73: Music and the Critique of Modern International Relations at the Annual Convention of the International Studies Association, Baltimore (USA), 22nd February 2017: Parts of Chapter Four draw on this paper and sections of "Music: Women Rewriting Punk Performance Politics" in the *Oxford Handbook of*

Politics and Performance, edited by S. Rai, S. Jestrovic, M. Gluhovic, and M. Saward. London/New York: Oxford University Press, 2021: 485-499

MIF
Amsterdam, April 2023

1. INTRO

To the Front

It is since 2010, with the publication of Patti Smith's prize-winning *Just Kids*, that a string of memoirs from an extraordinary group of *female* musicians has been grabbing centre stage. Spanning personal lives and public careers from the 1960's to present day, these accounts are an unapologetic recalibration of the burgeoning literature on *punk*; as an *ethos*, a self-identified sociopolitical *movement*, type of *music*, live *performance* practice, rebellious *subculture*, sonic and sartorial *aesthetic*. Like representatives of any cultural wave spearheaded by that era's youth, musicians whose careers straddle the official punk timeline have grown older. Some of those who made their way on stage – as part of punk's Do-It-Yourself (DIY) challenge to the commercial music establishment – are now published authors. Their public personae and creative output are integral to punk narratives of origins and disruption identified with high-profile acts, then and since. As part of an emergent cluster of singular writing these authors have bumped the music memoir business off its male-centric axis, redirecting public and critical attention from those penned by male (punk) music celebrities such as Peter Hook (Joy Division/New Order) or John Lydon/Johnny Rotten (Sex Pistols).

As an audible breakaway from the professionalized studio production values dominating pop music, in the 1970s, punk heralded a wave of sea changes in the sonics, performance practices, business model and audience expectations of mid-twentieth century Anglo-American music cultures. Characterized by the cliché 'play fast and loud' and the motto 'die young' (preferably before 25) punk, however defined, has diversified musically and geographically. Its proponents now span generations, as do audience demographics along race, class, gender, and religious lines, and across the spectrum of political affiliations. Literature about punk encompasses categories known as new wave, experimental/avant-garde electronica, post-punk, afro-punk, riot grrrl, and other derivations as these have flourished in their Anglo-American-European heartlands and around the world. Academic studies have also started to gather momentum with an increasing number from (former) punk exponents, if not fans, publications that work as a sort of meta-memoir to the first-hand narrative accounts.[1] The study considers women's music memoirs as formative contributions to shifting perceptions about women in public life after decades of studied disinterest, from mainstream academe and the music press. Considered together rather than pitted one against the other, the books are timely correctives to academic and trade literatures on the sociocultural, let alone political significance of any given musical moment that scandalously underplay the contribution of women who were there, making it happen. Such first-person accounts can inform debates about what it takes and means for a woman to make her way in any *masculinist* domain. The numerous, sometimes ironic, recollections of what it feels to be type cast, e.g., as girl-in-a-band, girl-band, woman-with-guitar, speak to the limitations of prominent recollections of the androgynous, gender-bending personae made famous by male celebrities and their bands.

In order of publication, here are the ten author-musicians: Patti Smith, Nina Hagen, Pauline Black (Belinda Magnus), Alice Bag (Alicia Armendariz), Viv Albertine, Kim Gordon, Carrie Brownstein, Chrissie Hynde, Britt Smith Start (Laura Salinger), and Cosey Fanni Tutti (Christine Newby). As women remain a numerical minority in all aspects of the music business, arts criticism and analysis, the authors revisit and so redress the standard historical narrative of *punk rock*: as white, working class (British in particular) aggressively 'male' rebelliousness, encapsulated in the *very* short, loud, fast, lo-fi and non-virtuoso track with brash, anti-establishment lyrical content, accompanied by the equivalent in confrontational behaviour on stage. As musicians their careers span the timeline demarcating the *broadening out* of punk music after its, for some, halcyon years in the late 1970s. The jury is still out on whether punk could ever have fulfilled its claim to be a revolutionary cultural vanguard. Women's punk memoir-writing opens up a rich vein of inquiry for students of politics, culture, and society into the *gendered* and, by association, *intersecting* race and class dimensions of punk's public archive (recordings, live shows, video footage, other memorabilia) and historiography (academic and journalist literatures).

The fifteen memoirs make for fascinating reading in their own right, as narratives – of intimate lives and public experiments in musicianship, artistic and professional collaborations – that buck the norm. But they are much more than stories of single-minded women achieving success in hostile domains.[2] The study considers the authors as creative agents, and through the prism of their own words it listens to some of the sounds they made. Taken together, the accounts make a substantive contribution to the sonic and literary archives of punk's pushback against the techno-economic values driving the business model through which the *global cultural industries* came of age in the twentieth century. High-profile acts from the UK and US punk scenes that have become anchored in popular imaginaries belie the depth of punk music's back catalogue and broader cultural legacy when considered through the eyes and ears of female musicians. Through the memoir idiom, authors evoke these intellectual concerns in a number of registers through their experience of punk's challenge to the sexual politics and political economic power that undergirds the Anglo-American music industry.

Figure 1: Carrie Brownstein
Artist: Mauricio Escobar (all rights reserved)

Beyond Fanstalgia

Punk rhetoric, ironic and serious, postures its challenge to the status-quo at full volume. Punk *musicking* remains indebted to articulating some sort of countercultural position and commitment to the communities that underpin the music-making, live and in the recording studio.[3] The first objective of this study is to listen more closely to some of the music the authors discuss. The memoirs are embedded in the process of making music itself, what it meant for authors as they challenged conventions about what counts as art, who gets to articulate the political moment, mood of the day, and who gets to play. The sonics and tools of musicological analysis tend to be avoided in studies of culture, society and politics conducted through the prism of the performing arts. Such an elision, empirical preference perhaps, belies how these scholarly and real-life domains are, in practice, intimately connected, despite an institutionalised separation into discrete disciplines. After all, historians also study musical topics as do media scholars, philosophers, psychologists, anthropologists, sociologists, and political scientists. Music researchers have been taking up a comparable interest in studying musical objects of analysis through the lens of culture, society and politics. In short, the overlaps between terms of reference and ways of conducting research offer more opportunities for garnering new knowledge and insights than do arcane divisions of labour and accreditation.

That said, the argument still needs reiterating, the public knowledge that emerges from questioning received wisdoms still needs pointing out, academic terms and references to scholarly debates do need introducing for other readerships. Not unlike how 'genres' sort diverse popular, and classical art music into recognized (and marketable) categories, disciplinary demarcation lines distinguish one academic research tradition from another; the division between the Humanities, Social Sciences, and 'hard' Sciences like engineering or physics is the most obvious though not the most insidious. When self-identifying as multi- or interdisciplinary a study (this is one such study) draws on and addresses more than one research tradition. Taking as a starting point that the interconnections between the study of culture, society and politics *requires* cross-disciplinary engagement is part of burgeoning university teaching and research that pushes back against disciplinary rigidities; against 'genres' so to speak. When it comes to explorations of the culture-society-politics nexus, the case of music for instance, the working premise is that the constitution of any political order, at the national or global level, includes the institutionalization of so-called norms and values (e.g. the civilizational, modernization ideals that undergird the former British Empire, Cold War standoffs, American hegemony, or the European Union's stress on liberal democracy and fundamental freedoms). Macro-level processes do not develop in a social, or cultural vacuum, however. It does not take long to notice the micro-level processes, sinews that connect political peaks 'upstream' to domains considered further 'downstream'; outside the purvey of political and economic power residing in legislatures or intergovernmental institutions, banks and stock markets. In some versions of the narrative-sweeps that populate work on 'Big History', 'Big Business', and 'Big Science', processes and relationships considered to take place 'downstream' become mere functions of such events 'higher up'; everyday life, cultural practices, familial or community relationships for instance.

Music making exemplifies the empirical interconnectivity between society, culture, and politics that academic 'disciplinary parochialism' cannot countenance. It does not take long to see and hear how powerholders are continually interfering in the lives and creative work of artists considered dissident or socially subversive. Those in power, governmental and cultural gatekeepers are prone to co-opt artists, musicians and composers in particular, for any number of political agendas; the exercise of 'soft power' through *cultural diplomacy* programmes has been the cornerstone of twentieth century geopolitics, and the precarious existence of the performing arts in times of war, civil strife, or militarised nationalism is all too palpable in the first decades of this century. Since its inception, punk's reception by incumbent powers-that-be and various moral guardians has epitomized the interplay between cultural politics and the (geo)politics of culture. Taking on board an auditory sense of how politics works in the world, as it co-creates the power dynamics framing people's lives, means taking the authors at their musical word by considering the sonics, the musicalities at stake. This is a departure from studies that impute political meaning directly from the lyric sheet, auto/biographical script, as analogy or metaphor in light of public-policy or political rhetoric. It means spending less time on the lyrics, as important as these can be for indexing content as political, on tabulating studio production values or theorizing about punk's psycho-emotional *affect* from the mosh pit.

Second, addressing punk as sound and politics, musical form and substance, performance and lifestyle recognizes the viscerality of how punk sets out to challenge any number of musical, societal and cultural norms. This is even more acute in the case of female exponents of punk repertoires and embodiments; e.g., the sexualized misdemeanour that may be attributed to a woman brandishing an electric guitar – lead or bass – on stage, or not singing 'nicely'. The authors have quite a lot to say about such stereotypes. In so doing they articulate, even if they do not answer, questions about whether the skewed sex-gender hierarchies in the arts – and in the political domains of public life and culture – can be undone by changing corporate ownership and control of recording, public attributions for the creative act (e.g. credits on album covers), copyright, and royalties. Accounts written by the women who wrote the songs, played and produced the records, organized the gigs, did the publicity, and formed the bands articulate the interconnections between the politics of everyday life, creative work, and current events; protagonists are the main acts in a shared, public retrospective. Episodes from the memoir-set capture women making music differently, against the norm, as well as making music on their own terms, despite but also with men. Their experiences challenge assumptions about whether music making and performance cultures like punk, which turn up the physical and emotional volume based on confrontational and physically ferocious forms of delivery are fundamentally male preserves.

The memoirists offer any number of viewpoints on such issues, adding grist to the mill of debates about how best to address the gender geopolitics of (mis)representation in public life. They throw into relief how women who persist in the music business do so against the odds, in an industry based on communities of practice that are skewed in favour of male proponents, and in literatures that focus on masculinities of performance, male-centric understandings of androgynous countercultures. They make their music, careers and relationships in the face of global, corporate forces of ownership and control that can appropriate and then remarket moments of resistance, artistic experimentation and innovation all too quickly. This genus of literature, first-hand accounts as, and of, performance articulates the ongoing disparities between how women in the political and cultural spheres are positioned and then portrayed by others vis-à-vis how they may regard or choose to depict themselves. The memoirs offer an additional dimension to inquiries into the 'norm or standard to which women's difference is being measured and so often found wanting. ... [and the work that] women do that is not typically regarded as political or politically interesting'.[4] This has relevance for how pundits and academic researchers consider the achievements of 'ordinary' (white) women, a minority, as opposed to 'exceptional' (black) women – even more a minority – who become famous at the intersection of cultural and political careers: for instance the former US Secretary of State under George W. Bush, Condoleezza Rice or Nina Simone both of whom had the talent and ambition to become a concert pianist (see Chapter Five).

Third, the study considers the memoir-based evidence in light of the incipient sex-gender stereotypes that continue to permeate music research and work on popular culture. Successive waves of feminist approaches alongside literary, cultural, or sonic 'turns' have shifted the terms of reference in longstanding discussions about whether a particular compositional or performance style can be regarded as intrinsically 'gendered'; innately 'masculine' or 'feminine'. As the debates about equal billing in music festivals and programming across the cultural spectrum continue, the authors' accounts, past and ongoing creative and public work have implications for how women's role in the cultural history and sex-gender politics of music-making can be reassessed. Hence asking questions such as 'where are the women?' and 'what do they have to say about punk as a cultural and political moment?' is a start, not an end in itself. The last decades of feminist-inspired music research include investigations into women as a demographic category of 'absenting' in the history of (western) popular music, gender as an analytical category (not simply a synonym for women), race/ethnicity and sexuality as constitutive components to making music, and writing about music; topics that all implicate a more rounded understanding of politics as a multidimensional study of power.[5]

It is precisely because they are penned by musicians talking about lives spent carving out an alternative, counter-intuitive place as independent artists, that the memoirs go further than affirming the need to address the entrenched absenting of "women as a group" from the official historiography and discography of any musical form, let alone self-identified, politically conscious ones such as punk. Abigail Gardner in her overview of a small selection of memoirs considers their primary drive as one of 'settling scores' in this regard.⁶ But this evaluation only works up to a point. There is a lot more going on within the pages, between the lines, and how the books speak to each other as authors address the work and public personae of any number of other, male, celebrities from their respective, and shared scenes. It is too reductionist because the tone of the publications taken as a composite whole is more exuberant than resentful. Women working as cultural agents in male-dominated fields, in this case music making, tell us something about how artists and/as consumers – fans and audiences, 'hear' and respond as gendered beings albeit in ways that cannot be reduced to biologized notions of sexual politics alone. Writing as musicians, audience members, fans and pundits the narratives resist and recalibrate received wisdoms, they do not merely reflect the sexualized and racialized dividing lines characterising the publishing and music business. These tensions, for artist and analyst alike, include the dynamics of denial, collusion, and confrontation given the geo-economic clout wielded by the global arts and entertainment industries, a domain in which streaming platforms have now staked their own, planetary claim for capturing artists' audiences and distribution channels. Music making, for commercial and non-commercial ends, and the blurred line between for what counts as success, is a political-cultural constellation that bespeaks multi-dimensional gatekeeping powers between state agencies, cultural institutions, and global corporate powers.

Fourth, the study considers the seemingly intransigent imbalance in who writes about, and about who makes what music in journalist and academic modes of analysis. To reiterate (repetition has its uses), making music and writing about music is, predominantly, still a male preserve. One way to get past this androcentric inertia is to take seriously how women's accounts change the terms of reference – and reverence – for their male counterparts. More so in the case of punk, however defined, which was – and continues to be – a musical form and cultural practice that embodies a politically charged sensibility, as sound, movement, and stage presence. However well it does or does not make good its ambitions to counter the power of the music majors, or to forge a space for gender/race and class-inclusive artistic practices, making music 'punk' implies a political stance, a project. After more than four decades of music making, fashion-lines, and material culture based on the improvisational, DIY, shoestring ethos that is intrinsic to punk, as a self-identified movement if not a brand, saying things out loud – loudly is but the start to figuring out why it matters to speak one's truth to power, at home, in the community or global spaces power is wielded. Authors like Carrie Brownstein, and Alice Bag who published her diaries of time spent with the Sandinistas in Nicaragua, put these levels of engagement into words as well as in their theories of punk musicking. Moreover, like the Clash, the Slits, or Sleater-Kinney and Sonic Youth in their day, members of the Pussy Riot collective mounted in 2012 a direct challenge not only to political but also cultural power in Russia through their deployment of punk idioms in theatre and sound.⁷

Given that women – whether it be in the arts and literature, in international affairs or business – are still in the minority it is really an 'open door' to want to look more closely at how women practitioners of punk idioms have managed to stand up to the bastions of power, of good taste (artistically), propriety (how should a grrrl in a band look or behave?) along the fracture lines of gender-race-class lines of acceptability. A study such as this one cannot answer these questions. Rather, it takes the authors and their complex subject matter as evidence of what it means to be part of a minority at the epicentre of *malestreamed* culture and politics.

What Makes Punk Music (Not)?

There have been many attempts at defining punk, as musical form and performance, 'style', counter-culture and, as it remains for a substantial section of academic and trade literature, the soundtrack of a social movement with roots in left-wing, anti-capitalist and anti-racist mobilization against the rise of the neoliberal, neo-conservative politics of Thatcher and Reagan as the 1970s morphed into the 1980s. Gzowski recognizes as soon as 1977, for instance, that in a '1976 article, journalist Caroline Coon was one of the first to use the term 'punk' to describe Britain's emerging underground rock scene. 'Punk rock' was initially coined in 1970 to characterize a group of late-1960s American rock bands'.[8] Helen Reddington, in her interview-based recovery of the 'lost women of rock music' during what she calls the 'punk era', refers to punk in a number of ways: as a sub-culture headlined by the Sex Pistols within a delineated time-period (1976-78); as a subculture with a 'uniquely therapeutic nature ... for a generation of unemployed people' made up of diverse 'micro-subcultures' that developed a 'musical and political interpretation of the punk idea which embraced a wide variety of people of both genders and varying ages; as a moment – a space – into which women in particular found their 'noisy', 'angry' voices, brandished instruments usually reserved for male (punk) rockers by giving women "unprecedented access to a voice and a platform." [9] Allusions to whether punk music is an American or British invention notwithstanding, Iggy Pop (born, James Newell Osterberg Jr.), object of desire, admiration, and disappointment for more than a couple of the authors here, had his tongue firmly in his cheek in an early interview on Canadian TV, recorded at the height of media headlines about punk rock's negative influence on youth. This is what Iggy had to say about definitions:

> 'Well, I'll tell you about punk rock. Punk rock is a word used by dilettantes and heartless manipulators about music that takes up the energies, and the bodies, and the hearts, and the souls, and the time, and the minds of young men [sic] who give what they have to it, who give everything they have to it. And it's a term based on contempt, it's a term that's based in fashion, style, elitism, Satanism, and every-

thing that's rotten about rock 'n' roll.... You see, what sounds to you like a load of trashy old noise is, in fact, the brilliant music of genius, myself and that music is so powerful that it's quite beyond my control...' (Iggy Pop, 1977)[10]

Iggy's disdain remains alive and well today, as does his ironic 'humble-bragging' as he takes to task the industry of *genrification* linked to commercial success against which 'first generation' punks railed. The role of dress, bodies, and movement on stage are not absent from the memoirs, nonetheless. Reflections on punk adornments ('clothes, clothes, clothes' as evoked in the title of Albertine's first memoir), body image, or musical aptitude feature. But a sartorial – image or branding – aspect is but one. The weight of analysis, retrospection engages the reader with the tracks: short songs where performers revelled in, or agonized over their rudimentary technique (beginner guitarists); acoustics based on volume up loud; lyrics shouted or sung deliberately out of tune about topics that were anything but love songs and which included odes to (violent) insurrection, refusal to conform, calls to revolution, political stances on current events of the day (anti-war, anti-establishment, anti-monarchy). The cast of personae whose monikers have become synonymous with punk also feature: e.g. Johnny Rotten, Poly Styrene, Sid Vicious as do prototypical bands with names conjuring up bodily fluids (the Buzzcocks), decay (Rancid), sex (the Sex Pistols), confrontation (the Clash), nihilism (the Damned, Bikini Kill) and death (Dead Kennedys), body parts (the Slits, Stiff Little Fingers). The musician-authors of the books in question here provide fresh insights and energy into a period, and its afterlife in music journalism, including the never-ending release of *manmoirs* from pop-punk-rock male celebrities.

Punk as a *musical* expression, and demarcated timeline of sonic revolt since its public entrée in the 1970s, is straightforward in its ideal type; locatable in those first years as based on less than three-minute tracks (sometimes less than a minute), fast, thrashed guitars, three-chord (max) harmonies for bass or lead guitar. Vocals less sung than yelled, staging basic, audience and performers interacting through the mosh-pit, mixed spittle, flying beer bottles, mutual gestures and verbalizations of abuse, sweat and physicality in which bodies crashed into one another, crushed forward, jumped up and down. Yet this very image is, in itself, a form of *fanstalgia*. Ian Penman is one pundit who exemplifies this tension between punk as a generic or exclusive term. He cites Solange Knowles, who evokes punk as a form through which artists are 'allowed to be and rage and express anger, be anti-establishment...' in her review of the book *Why Solange Matters* by Stephanie Phillips. Penman sees such evocations as the antithesis of punk which for him conjures up the 'glowering skyline of a 1970s UK council estate.'[11] In this view, more inclusive evocations of 'punk' is what 'punk' is 'not'. Penman laments, in effect, that punk "means now whatever anyone wants or wills" particularly when African American artists from the post-rap/R&B artists generation such as Solange Knowles take the term on to describe their own sense of non-compliance. Penman overlooks that punk's 'towering skylines' of working-class British (male) culture is also an ideal type. As punk era artists-cum-authors such as Helen Reddington, Cosey Fanni Tutti, Alice Bag, and Pauline Black point out, punkish attributes emerged from a range of skylines, suburban or inner-city poverty, race and gender lines of experimentation and demarcation. For Penman 'it may come as a surprise to some that 'punk' can still be brandished like this, as an outsider ethic, a gloriously unsafe safe-place for experiment and play, rage and reclamation.'[12] It bears noting that rap and hip-hop artists, who emerged in the same decade as British punk acts such as the Sex Pistols or the Clash, were also generating their music from a DIY, not-strictly-commercial sensibility. In their historical synchronicity we can hear echoes of Solange's appropriation of the term *punk* to denote a particular *attitude*, one that pushes back against entrenched societal and industry norms across race, class, and gender lines.

By the same token the diversity and stubbornness of the authors' personal accounts, and their public output cannot be confined either to reductionist tropes around femininity versus masculinity, or the policy politics of demographic representativeness. How they made, and still make music, alongside their many other pursuits resonates with successive generations of academic debates about how sex-gender roles can be seen and heard at work in public life and culture. Which leaves us with an open-ended query; do any of these women and the bands they took part in, founded and led, really qualify as strictly-*punk*? Which definition best encapsulates these diverse acts if not punk (sub-categorizations aside)? Anglo-centric critics such as Penman would say not. Indeed, he questions whether American acts such as Sleater-Kinney (Carrie Brownstein) or Sonic Youth (Kim Gordon) can be termed punk at all. Yet this he does whilst decrying the dangers of 'purism, a conservatism that repels anything new or different and instead fetishizes micro-differences of style and caste.'[13] Debates, ongoing, about commercial but also political and philosophical definitions pivot on the understandings that *culture* matters. Moreover, the links between punkish-sounding bands, right-wing skinhead scenes, left-wing politics, and religious fervour are also a part of punk discographies. This too is a question about the intimacies between culture and politics, society and the arts along the sinews that connect the local and global dimensions of action.

Where punk begins and ends as a political sensibility in the literature to date tends to rest on odes paid to the engaged lyrics and public positions of male figures in the punk pantheon, such as Joe Strummer from the Clash. The women whose music features in the memoir-set are lyricists as well as composers. Viv Albertine notes, in a reflection on what she thinks the Slits stood for, how their 'lyrics were very carefully thought about and scrutinized. No peddling clichés and lies for us. No lazy escapism. Words have to be true to your life. Write about what you know. And make people think.'[14] Later generations of punk artists are less focused on about political delineations along the lyric sheet alone, Katie Alice Greer, for instance, from Priests, an exponent of the 'new "new wave" of self-identifying punk bands, argues that 'everything is political, and music is inherently part of politics.'[15] Helen Reddington's account, her own and that of her interviewees, of punk as *synonymous* with 'music-making by empowered women' is tinged with disillusionment in light of how the music press, at the time and since, is steeped in a 'male memory' that is, moreover, 'metrocentric'.[16] Her critique is also aimed at high-profile scholarly and journalist chroniclers of the punk period that continue to ignore, mute, or under-estimate the role that women have played as musicians, producers, and writers. Reddington devotes her penultimate chapter to this issue of male/masculinist gatekeepers who continue to dominate the historiography, play lists, and airtime; Anglo-American interlocuters in particular. How exactly some music is consciously, or unintentionally positioned as "political." the sex-gender power relations inherent in respective appellations, is an historical as well as an analytical question since the first wave of feminist revisions of the classical music canon in the 1990s.[17] Engaging with how musicians, particularly those seldom given any airplay or column-space such as women (sad but true), discuss these issues as first-hand accounts provides a fresh impulse, some additional complexity to these debates.

Figure 2: Brix Smith Start
Artist: Mauricio Escobar (all rights reserved)

Reader Notes

Four points of entry frame the study: the books, their authors, the historical context, and musical output. It includes some focus on the musical material to get closer to the authors' own accounts of how they made their music as beginners and more experienced musicians.[18] Whilst a memoir is, by any definition, a manufactured reconstruction of a life or stage in one's life the authors do focus on the music they made, when starting out as, nominally, punk acts and the ways in which they and their creative practices developed over time. Hence music making, and attitudes to the business and creative impulses feature in different ways and at different levels of formal writing about technical production values and processes, learning how to play, and then perfecting a particular technique on an instrument – usually the (bass) guitar, or discovering vocal attributes. Authors span the spectrum, celebrated and heralded by punk, as absolute beginner, relative adept in another instrument; for instance, Pauline Black, frontwoman and vocalist from the 2-tone band, the Selecter played piano at quite an advanced level when starting out.

But why does it matter to incorporate close listening time into the study? I would argue that getting inside the way a piece of music is put together does change the way you hear and so experience its sonic composition. Some may argue this analytical focus affects the enjoyment of the listening experience or is too strenuous for lay people. It need not. Nor does it mean having to have a music degree, be able to read music, or be a virtuoso performer. Punk's breakthrough was to claim creative and performance space for the novice musician within its sonic register and despite the demands of professionalized music promotion. As proponents show, making music can also break through the sound barriers of expertise based on racialized and sexualized hierarchies of cultural worth(iness). So can listening.

There are some conceptual lines of inquiry, familiar to academic readers, which will make their appearance in each chapter. One notion that undergirds the methodological approach for this study is the notion of *intersectionality*: a way to connect often disparate topics through unpacking the multiple dimensions to how individuals and communities make sense of their worlds and, conversely, can become defined in powerful others' preconceived ideas; such as those about sex-gender roles. Considering how racialised and sexualized stereotypes combine in lived lives, and institutions, generates work on the multiplicity of discriminatory sites and discourses, towards a group (e.g. black queer women), a demographic (e.g. women in the arts let alone women from ethnic minorities in the arts), or a scholarly discipline. References to intersectionality are not to imply a flattening out of distinct, embedded power differentials along singular axes such as race (prominent in US debates) or class (a focus in the UK). Rather, the term highlights the *nuances* of experience and success, commercial and critical, that the artists have experienced, as individuals and communities. These turn differently on crisscrossing, always moving contexts of possibility around race, class, wealth, and networks in the case of women in music, whose 'gender and sexual [and racial] unruliness' becomes political subject matter, to paraphrase Judith Peraino.[19]

Memoirists Chrissie Hynde, Nina Hagen, Alice Bag, Pauline Black, Patti Smith to some extent, and Carrie Brownstein in particular, write about the interplay between the historical times, local and global political events, and respective sex-gender power dynamics that formed them as well as those mentors, musicians and artists that influenced them when considering their own creative practices and pathways. Rather than infer official ideological positions from any author, when not stated explicitly (more on such points in Chapter Five) I draw out some of the conceptual connections between the music-making, historical and political contexts to which the author may, or may not refer, and wider debates around the politics of art, art and politics, and music as a vehicle for social change.

Which Books and Why

It is a booming corner of the publishing industry, the *femoir* and in particular the *rock-femoir*. So which books to consider, which to leave out? The selection here is not entirely arbitrary. Chapter Two looks more closely at similarities and differences (in authorial voice, style, narrative structures) and deployment of an author's personal papers – diaries, photos, fan memorabilia- along with other secondary sources reflect the thirty years spanning the authors' ages, *geocultural* locales and their own sense of, well, destiny (if you like). That said, this is not a comparative study. Nor is it a critical review. References to other prominent memoirists such Nina Simone (born, Eunice Kathleen Waymon) and Simone de Beauvoir offer some additional lateral insights into first-hand recollections of being there, at the time.

Around 2014 the music press, and major public cultural spaces such as the Tate Modern in London, were gearing up to commemorate the fortieth anniversary of punk rock's 'arrival' in the late nineteen-seventies, sweeping away the hi-fi production values, virtuosity and long windedness of 'prog-rock', the slick studio recordings of the pop-music charts, in its wake. Much has been written about punk in the mid to late seventies as it emerged in the UK through the fame of the Sex Pistols, and its centres of gravity in the US, New York and Detroit, with acts such as the New York Dolls, Iggy Pop and the Stooges around the same time, followed closely, as standard accounts go, with bands such as Blondie, Talking Heads, Devo, and others.[20] Here too differences exceed similarities. The fifteen memoirs studied were published between 2010-2022 with nearly half of them appearing in

2014-2016; a steady flow of memoirs annually for twelve years in this sub-category, of women writing about music as musicians, alone.

So, let's start at the beginning in terms of publication dates: In 2010 Patti Smith's memoir, *Just Kids*, of her early years living with the photographer Robert Mapplethorpe (1946-1989) as a budding romantic/beat generation poet and starting-out performance artist/rock vocalist, won the 2010 National Book Award in the US. The celebrity status of both Smith (b. 1946) and her former life-companion Mapplethorpe in American mid-20th century high-pop cultural life, set the bar for memoirs from women in punk/rock from that point on. It also sets out the lines of demarcation about how best to define 'punk', as discussed. For while Smith is considered the 'godmother' of punk rock, her music is not, strictly speaking, punk; at least not when compared to the output of others in this study. In addition, Patti Smith features as an object of desire, fandom, and aspiration in several of these books; her influence, and stage persona are immortalized by Viv Albertine, Chrissie Hynde, Alice Bag, and also Nina Hagen, as a performance role-model, proto-punk icon. Smith considers herself, at least in *Just Kids*, as a poet first, a singer in a rock 'n' roll band second. It is her second book, *M Train*, that makes clear how she sees her music career in light of her poetry, visual practice (photography and painting), and writing. Her personal life is less enunciated, alluded to by names and events (often their death). Subsequent memoirs, such as *M Train*, published in 2015, and *Year of the Monkey* from 2019 take on a more meta-level approach to the act of 'memoirizing', with the creative act of musicking, and those musicians with whom she has worked (including her late husband Fred Smith, and daughter, Jesse Paris Smith) more as backdrops to the topic at hand; the act of writing itself in the autobiographical voice.

Viv Albertine's first memoir, of her time with the Slits, considered one of the UK's most significant bands of punk's establishment in the late seventies-early eighties, *Clothes, Clothes, Clothes, Music, Music, Music, Boys, Boys, Boys* was published in 2014. Her second book, focusing on her relationship with her mother, father, and sister, *To Throw Away Unopened*, came out in 2018. In 2015, Kim Gordon, bassist in the American, 'indie', or 'alt-rock' band, Sonic Youth, published her memoir entitled *Girl in a Band*. 2015 saw the publication of *Hunger Makes me a Modern Girl* from Carrie Brownstein, from a prominent band in the US-based *riot grrrl* (punk-inspired) musico-feminist wave from the 'nineties, Sleater-Kinney. And in 2016 two memoirs emerged; first Brix Smith Start's reconstruction of her time before, during, and after playing, and living with the indefinable Manchester-based, meta-punk band, the Fall and its frontman Mark E. Smith (1957-2018) in *The Rise, The Fall, and The Rise*. Second is Chrissie Hynde's account of her beginnings, and subsequent rise to fame in *Reckless: My Life as a Pretender*. Both Smith Start and Hynde made their professional lives, as Americans, in the

UK. By 2017 Cosey Fanni Tutti (the stage name for Christine Newby) had published her memoir – *Art, Sex, Music* – on life as a member of the performance art/experimental sonics collective of counter-cultural 'noiseniks', Throbbing Gristle, based in from Hull (UK) and her later career as part of the electronic duo, Chris and Cosey.[21] Cosey's second book, *Re-Sisters*, was published in 2022. Musically the authors and their various bands span the spectrum of what could be considered 'punk', if not in form and delivery then in attitude towards the mainstream music industry. Some are close friends and collaborators, others know (of) each other from a distance, have toured and played together, been at each other's gigs.

Three other musicians' memoirs complete the set with books published in 2011; Alice Bag (stage name for Alicia Armendariz, born 1958) who fronted the LA based punk band, the Bags with her first 2011 memoir entitled *Violence Girl: East L.A. Rage to Hollywood Stage, a Chicana Punk Story*. The other memoir from that year, also following close behind Patti Smith's *Just Kids*, is Pauline Black's *Black By Design: A 2-Tone Memoir*. Black (born Belinda Magnus in 1953) recounts her life as front woman of the 2-tone (ska) band, the Selecter from the perspective of a mixed race performer who, like Bag, made her mark in music scenes dominated by (white) men and, as is the case with our other memoirists, white women. Third, Nina Hagen's memoir, not available in English, takes the reader through her upbringing in an artistic, non-conformist family in East Germany to her rise to fame in western Europe and her encounters with the first generation of British punk bands in London. Patti Smith is the oldest, born in 1946 with her first memoir published when she was in her sixties. Brix Smith Start and Carrie Brownstein are the youngest, born in 1962 and 1974 respectively. Chrissie Hynde, Cosey Fanni Tutti, Kim Gordon, Pauline Black, and Viv Albertine were all born in the early-to-mid fifties (1951, 1951, 1953, 1953, and 1954). Nina Hagen was born in 1955, Alice Bag in 1958. Dates of birth clustered around the early 'fifties notwithstanding, this line-up places Brownstein's memoir from 2015 as the one penned by the youngest memoirist, barely in her forties at date of publication. As authors, and exponents of first-generation (1970s) and second/third generation (1980s hardcore/1990s riot grrrls) punk, these ten women lend their authoritative voice to the burgeoning literature on punk countercultures and music scenes.

Who does not make this cut? The most prominent in terms of global reach is Debbie Harry's *Face it: A Memoir* from 2019 which is about her band Blondie, neither a self-authored nor a substantial autobiographical narrative. Rather it is a compilation of conversations with Sylvie Simmons fleshed out with copious photos and fan-portraits of Harry, from Harry's personal archives. Even though Harry (born Angela Trimble in 1945) is the same age as several other authors, marginally older than Patti Smith, and Blondie is considered by pundits as one of the most iconic US punk/new wave bands, a line in the sand has to be drawn somewhere. By the same token I draw on Nina Simone's memoir, also ghost-written but, nonetheless, a substantive autobiographical account of Simone's creative and political vision. Why Simone, a Black political activist and innovator of socially conscious blues, jazz and gospel crossovers from a previous generation, features in a study of punk women's memoirs will be explained in due course. Included in this written text is a gallery of portraits from the French-Columbian artist Mauricio Escobar. Working on the basis of public domain images as 'found' source material, Escobar has allowed himself to be inspired by the musician-memoirists' public personae; not only in their younger years but also in more recent times. He has worked with charcoal and a primary colour palette developing his own vision of the memoirists as a group. Escobar notes that as we worked together, he:

> 'opted for a simple technique, basic materials such as charcoal and darker colours, working in a figurative style that does not copy public images but, rather, works with my perception of each woman's, each musician's personality through the photographic medium. ... I chose two or three for each individual from different periods, synthesizing certain characteristics – not to reproduce the shot as an exact facsimile – but, most importantly, to convey my sense of their personality, always a complicated and complex notion, that they exude from the images, and that speaks to me.'[22]

Figure 3: Diptych – Cosey Fanni Tutti and Viv Albertine
Artist: Mauricio Escobar (all rights reserved)

Escobar's work provides a visual dimension to the thousands of words under examination here alongside the many hours of music recordings, video footage and other creative work in the public (online and offline) domain. The portraits have been curated as an ongoing conversation during the conception and writing of this book, a form of mutual inspiration to get things done on the basis of intuition and increased knowledge of what animates the authors in all their endeavours. I am indebted to Mauricio for his commitment and contribution to the study with a visual artist's impressions of the musicians.

Chapter Outline

The next five chapters proceed as follows: Chapter Two delves more into the form and substance of the memoir-set. Clustering fifteen memoirs from ten authors, already marketed as a subset of the rock memoir genre, together for the purposes of study begs comparisons. Contrasts in style, aesthetic and political sensibility, musical tastes and attitudes to commercial success, or lack thereof are also considered as a composite portrait of the books. The argument is that these publications need to be treated as a substantial public archive for scholars of the politics of contemporary musico-cultural movements, of which punk is one. In an industry dominated by men, the publication of first-hand accounts by influential, and high-profile musicians who are women about a shared period of musical innovation matters for public record, and for scholarship. Politically this is a feminist issue as much as it is an empirical shift in the timeline and point-of-view for *punkographies* to date. The selection criteria, and how I curated themes for the subsequent chapters provide the research rationale (more in Chapter Six for the methodologically curious). In Chapter Three, *voice* is the main theme for considering how Patti Smith, Nina Hagen, Alice Bag, and Brix Smith Start write about finding their own voice; as vocalists and figuratively as they strike out into public performance. Passages from the respective memoirs provide insights into how they developed their own performance repertories, usually through trial and error. We pay a first visit to the thought of Roland Barthes, a philosopher who was writing about music as art and practice in the same period that Patti Smith was first performing her Rimbaud-inflected spoken-word, proto-punk shows in New York

The guitar, and women playing guitar, is the main theme for Chapter Four. Authors have a lot to say in this regard as they confront their own preconceptions about female bodies on stage, as guitar players and learning to play the instrument of popular music's male guitar heroes for the first time. Roland Barthes' ideas about music as an *embodied* practice provide ways into thinking about why punk made such a mark at the time and women playing guitar fast and loud in particular; commonplace now but in the 1970s and 1980s not the case. What constitutes 'good' punk performance values provides a counterweight to some of the mythologies about punk through how prominent exponents changed the way guitar was played, and how it sounded. The penultimate chapter, Chapter Five, considers several not-strictly-musical themes, including more recent undertakings from the authors since publishing the memoirs in the set. We return to the question about whether aging, for women in particular, plays a particular role for women looking to have their say in public recollections, if not commemorations of the hopefulness for sociocultural change that punk, along with concomitant music scenes such as reggae, ska and 2-tone sounded. Topics such as loss, sexual mores, racism, discrimination in the artworld and public media, and gender-based violence return from initial considerations in Chapter Two. All the authors have continued to create, music and literature, and in other formats such as the visual arts, television, theatre, and poetry. The chapter ends with a reflection on why Nina Simone is pertinent to the study. I consider her as the one who did it first in terms of the punk attitude to audience, public approval, and fame, all of which comprise combative relationships between the artist, her audience, fans and critics. Some recapitulation, some extrapolations, and some further delineations are the themes in Chapter Six, the *outro*.

Setting Out

Much more than a publishing gimmick, the music memoirs – a subset of a larger literature – penned by these women provide new knowledge of how the music was made in the 'punk era'. They offer fresh insights into the process of song writing in terms of lyrics, melody, and sound production; from a formulaic 'pop-song' approach to the improvised and experimental. We are reading about music-making from inside the process. The authors are not onlookers. They are describing the emotional, physical, and creative paths they took to make their music, and what making that music meant to their lives, at the time and since. They are also providing a multi-layered account of overlapping cultural and political movements that are embedded in their respective *musicking*. Reading the books together, as a complex whole but also each on their own musical and lyrical terms, provides a rich vein of inquiry for further research. But they are also a treat for fans and pundits; past, present and future.

2. MUSICIANS AS MEMOIRISTS

Punk Performance Sexual Politics

'As a child I thought I would never grow up, that I could will it so. And then I realized, quite recently, that I had crossed some line, unconsciously cloaked in my chronology. How did we get so damn old?' (Patti Smith)[23]

Female musicians publishing their memoirs, now established musicians, and whose work is identified with punk started out, more often than not, as complete novices. The spirit of DIY animates all these accounts; an ethos, at the time and since, pivoting on a 'public image' that embodies, and intones *DIY* as both ad hoc improvisation and a strategic repertoire of anti-establishment *performance* practices.[24] They present to the reader a multifaceted, redacted peek into their lives, and those with whom they worked and lived through various incarnations, punk and 'post-punk'; as not only authors but also visual artists, scriptwriters, fashion designers, television personalities, poets, and producers. All continue to perform and create music, solo or in various ensembles. The memoirs depict their authors' respective musical comings of age over a period from the 1960s through to present day; times that have seen waves of feminist politics, civil rights, and musical challenges to the political economic and sociocultural status quo.[25]

Authors provide recollections of their own engagement in political mobilization if not counter-cultural provocations: For example; Cosey Fanni Tutti's work with Throbbing Gristle's 'shock and awe' street happenings and her 'Sex' show at the ICA in London (see Chapter Five), Alice Bag's trip to Sandinista Nicaragua, Pauline Black's engagement with anti-racism movements, the *2-tone movement* being a musical iteration thereof, during and since her coming to prominence as front woman for the Selecter, Nina Hagen's rejection of the East German regime's cultural codes growing up in a family replete with public figures as she became a star herself, on both sides of the Cold War East-West divide. Author-musicians variously self-identify, however pundits may have positioned them over time, as participants in the wave of 'punk' sonic rebellion against corporate control over music-making and distribution. Their autobiographical accounts map diverse sources of inspiration that come from a wide range of other musical sources, popular culture and literature. They acknowledge their contemporaneous, mutual presence through recollections of performing – and partying – with each other, as protagonists in overlapping musico-subcultural scenes, photo shoots, as they provide their respective takes on the iconic episodes that have become part of the (un)official fabric of punk's audio-visual and written-word public archive. The music made, then and now, live and in the studio, co-constitutes the 'inter-related discursive and embodied practices' of punk's *public performance politics*.[26]

The memoir content and authors' views on feminism can be disconcerting for readers and scholars identifying as feminist who presume the artists to be natural allies in advocating women's rights in general or feminist research, and political agendas in particular; more on these subtexts in due course. A case in point is reviewers' responses to Chrissie Hynde's account of her experience of being (gang) raped in *Reckless*, swift in their condemnation of Hynde's expression of regret about what she could have done to avoid the attack.[27] Read the passage carefully, however, and think between the lines of Hynde's self-admonishment in light of how rape survivors may choose to voice their experiences (in an off-hand way being one), if at all. This is similar to other episodes of intimate partner abuse in some accounts; Brix Smith Start raises an equivalent experience in another register when revealing a buried experience of date-rape. And then there is Viv Albertine's harrowing description of her experience while on a date as what started out as consensual turned nasty and descended into assault along with Cosey Fanni Tutti's revelations in both her memoirs about the abusive dimensions to her long-term relationship with Throbbing Gristle co-founder Genesis P-Orridge.[28] Pauline Black, in her memoir *Black By Design*, reveals how she was systematically molested as a young child (from the age of nine) by a neighbour for a considerable length of time, forced to see the perpetrator for years living next door even after having had the courage to tell someone about what was happening to her.[29] Black, like Hynde, is explicit about what happened. Even though she states that the molestation was not rape as such (legal distinctions in different jurisdictions notwithstanding), Black's account puts her trauma immediately into the wider societal context of sexual politics at the time but also, sadly, nowadays:

> 'When I hear the stories of other abuse sufferers I am always staggered by the everyday nature of the crime. It is not that you are captured in the street and dragged off into the undergrowth and raped, that would be bearable almost, because you could prove to everybody that a crime had been committed, but when an adult man French kisses and intimately touches a child, that is not something that leaves tangible evidence. It is not something that a child can put a name to. That is the tragedy. The only evidence is the invisible mental scar. That is the crime.'[30]

What is striking about the above examples as told by Albertine, Hynde, Cosey Fanni Tutti, or Black for instance is how the encounters are woven into the autobiographical narrative in ways that do not reduce their narrators to victimhood, to feminine stereotypes and sexual politics tropes that position women artists as more prone to violence or mistreatment from others. Patti Smith for instance relates an incident, in *Just Kids* as well as various interviews, when she barely knew Robert Mapplethorpe of being (possibly) propositioned by an older male stranger in New York with a sense of self-deprecating humour; Robert Mapplethorpe is credited as an unlikely saviour from an awkward encounter as Smith recalls what her mother told her about talking to strangers. When race, gender, and class intersect as a life, as is the case with Pauline Black or Alice Bag, the narratives provide an added dimension to the punk timeline, given its white/male/working-class profile. For Black, intersections of discrimination and exclusion are also indices of empowerment and mobilization against conservative, far right political platforms: She ends her memoir with the call that this 'woman is not for resigning!'[31] Here Nina Simone sets the tone in another register as she recollects some of the darker episodes in her (love and professional) life. Simone's memoir is a mix of self-assuredness that comes with her awareness of her public persona and musico-political trajectory as a prominent civil rights activist, yet who still found herself pushed around by recording companies and unscrupulous managers. Whether or not Simone liked being referred to as 'difficult' she acknowledges her own proclivity to castigate audiences if they did not respond to her performance standards.[32] Her life-story, as reflected in her autobiographical account, numerous documentaries and biographies is a striking example of this double-edginess to women writing about domestic violence, emotional and mental health issues, and their own misbehaviour in retrospect.[33] I will return to the notion that Nina Simone could be regarded as a punk pioneer in some key respects in Chapter Five.

In terms of punk women recalling comparable episodes, I would ask reader-cum-critic to tread lightly on other women's traumas, particularly given how 'everyday' violence against women continues around the world: UN Women report that 'globally, an estimated 736 million women – almost one in three – have been subjected to physical and/or sexual intimate partner violence, non-partner sexual violence, or both at least once in their life (30 per cent of women aged 15 and older). This figure does not include sexual harassment.' These figures are corroborated by the World Health Organization in reports underscoring how "intimate partner violence" makes up the bulk of statistics ... a major public health problem and a violation of women's human rights.'[34] Moreover, when a person's memoir becomes fodder for censure in the digital networked context in which memoirs are now written and consumed, the ringtones of indignation about such episodes feed the commercial dynamics of algorithmically driven *circuits of culture* that nourish "blame the victim" tropes.

Indeed, many *punkographies* are retrospective surveys, penned by male (yes, mostly men) music journalist-protagonists who cut their teeth in the respective scenes: Julien Temple (with Malcolm McLaren) and Jon Savage, Paul Morley and the Manchester scene through the life and times of the band Joy Division and its successor, New Order, or Danny Boyle's mini-series on the Sex Pistols.[35] These influential historical accounts have been formative in prominent representations of punk – as an era, cultural movement, and cast of characters: Simon Reynolds observes, in his melancholy review of a biography of Malcolm McLaren, punk impresario and former manager of the Sex Pistols, that McLaren's take on punk-as-branding was based on a particular 'sense of fashion' that exploited the tropes of 'sex, style and subversion' in order to shock audiences in the, then, TV-dominated public spaces. The Malcolm McLaren and Vivienne Westwood fashion lines, branded as 'SEX', have been formative in how punk emerged as a sartorial and sonic practice, according to Reynolds doomed to 'commit some kind of outrage, through clothes, language or imagery, and then scorn the revulsion they had sought and achieved. The only thing that could thwart them was acceptance.'[36]

There is a lot more to say about punk and/as fashion, a topic the memoirists explore as well (see Chapter Five). The death of Jordan (born Patricia Rooke), member of Vivienne Westwood's team at SEX and 'punk rock fashion icon', in 2022 at the age of 66 underscores the extra-sonic dimensions to punk sensibilities.[37] Fan-stalgia tinged with regret also characterize academic publications on this generation, a body of literature that straddles disciplines such as cultural studies, sociology, popular music research, media and communications, and politics – and feminist sub-fields thereof. When it comes to women and/as punk musicians the question that goes begging is whether or not it is pertinent to bemoan how 'many of us are still attached to the fables of punk, these stories we can't stop retelling' are doomed to 'become incomprehensible to young people, requiring too much historical backfilling to be worth the effort'. Women's underlit roles as leading figures in such, androcentric 'fables' must temper the middle-aged, masculinist notion that punk has had its day, that it is time 'to leave the twentieth century, and leave punk behind there with it' simply because the Sex Pistols are no more, and neither is Malcolm McLaren.[38]

In the context of the roll-call of male versus female representation in burgeoning literary and audio-visual punkographies, recall an observation from Chapter One: namely, those women who 'make it' challenge not only malestream nods to their formative role, musical prowess and contribution, but also some prevalent feminist categories of significance. This is because as women who perform punk the authors buck the masculinist and exceptionalist tropes through which punk has been framed in public discourses. A number of memoirists tend to present their careers as part of "ordinary" live-paths and aspirations (Viv Albertine in particular though this is not the case for Cosey Fanni Tutti or Nina Hagen) nonetheless.

In both instances, generalizations about what their career-paths indicate about all women in music belies their 'gender and sexual [and racial] unruliness' when considered as tools for both research and political agendas.[39] Such unruliness is not reserved for "strictly-punk" acts either: in recent years, the African American artist Beyoncé has become an *influencer*, a (self-managed) global brand that now coincides with the kudos her celebrity status has lent to the Black Lives Matter movement. For the decade following the emergence of punk, pop icon Madonna played a documented role in reshaping the academic canon on women in music through her appropriation of some punkish dress styles (which the Slits made their own), mixed with her deployment of hyper-femininity and sexually explicit iconography (outfits, videos, lyrical hooks such as 'like a virgin') in her glory days in the 1980s. Whatever one's expectations, these accounts provide much to consider about the personal-political costs, and investments involved when women go against the grain of the gender-power politics 'stoking the star-making machinery behind the popular song.'[40]

Punk Public Archives

> 'I regret half of this story and the other half is the sound you heard.' (Chrissie Hynde)[41]

The timeframe in which most of the memoirs were published converges with the putative fortieth anniversary of punk as a self-aware and self-referential musico-cultural 'movement'; at least in terms of British punk acts, the Sex Pistols in particular whose album *Never Mind the Bollocks Here's the Sex Pistols* was released in 1977, serve as the primary reference point. The shared time-window and overlapping dates of publication underscore some of the personal, professional and political interconnections between authors despite immediate differences in age, family backgrounds, and the stylistic diversity in their music-making as well as literary and artistic sensibilities. The bands that provide the platform for the authors' punk entrée are the Slits (Viv Albertine), the Pretenders (Chrissie Hynde), Sonic Youth (Kim Gordon), Sleater-Kinney (Carrie Brownstein), the Selecter (Pauline Black) and the Fall (Brix Smith Start). As for Patti Smith, the Patti Smith Band overlaps the timeframe in *Just Kids*, the first of her memoirs while for Nina Hagen, christening her band the Nina Hagen Band was not unanimously accepted by her bandmates. The Bags was the name of just one of the bands that Alice Bag headed up, their back catalogue and profile marked by several tracks only. Cosey Fanni Tutti's contribution to her signature collectives, COUM and Throbbing Gristle, drives her memoir's chronology as does her complex 'off-and-on' relationship (creative and personal) with co-founder Genesis P-Orridge and subsequent partnership with Chris Carter with whom she still lives, and performs as Chris and Cosey.[42]

In the Third Person

A striking feature of both music journalism (high-profile authors of regular columns and long-read essays) and music scholarship as an academic pursuit is the merging of practitioner with researcher-commentator perspectives. Many authors on music matters, musicians, or particular periods in these domains are or have been musicians themselves if not directly involved in the sector in other capacities. The amalgamation of voice for academic treatments of punk music politics, first person resonating as third person, is part of the assumed authority that comes with references to a career in music, past or present. These associations depart from standard academic practice and affiliations, sketched in Chapter One, in which claims of expertise are to be based on years of specialist training, evidence of 'objectivity' and methodological rigour ('scientific' methods) along any given disciplinary pathway; laboratory experiments to mathematics, to anthropological fieldwork, to philosophical reflection. The mixing of passion – emotional attachment – for a research topic or discipline is considered in some quarters as undermining academic notions of veracity.

Those writing on topics considered "low" or popular culture (take computer games, comics, popular TV, mainstream pop music for instance), and some who study "high" culture (such as literature, theatre, cinema) can stand accused of being 'pseudo-intellectuals', self-indulgent in their exploration of themes about which they are openly enthusiastic. Passion for one's object of research is according to this view "not done." patent enthusiasm for one's topic or area of expertise considered a dereliction of scholarly duty, bad taste according to defenders of academic decorum. The elevation of the third person perspective – objective, dispassionate, measured – and its sidekick, the Royal We (academic writing often uses 'we' in order to avoid the perceived hazards of explicit ownership and authorship of the first person, 'I') still presumes mutuality. When it comes to writing about the arts and culture, even within these topics' home grounds such as musicology or art history, the dispassionate third voice effectively cloaks the psycho-emotional investment that academics-cum-punk-practitioners have in their object of study. The permission that the first-person grants when authoring a memoir is not provided. Yet, threaded throughout the historiography and pedagogy that comprise centuries of theoretical treatises on western, classical art and popular music as form, content, and meaning along with those bodies of music theory that address the Arab world and classical Indian (North and South Indian) schools of musical performance)[43] are authors who are also practitioners; leading adepts in some cases of the musical tradition, theoretical or performance school in question.

This double-life runs through the research literature focusing on punk/punk-derived themes, including women's under-valued role in this particular period, for there are authors whose own careers straddle their punk and their academic careers. Others are openly avid fans, relatives, or can attest to having 'been there too'.[44] Three authors are pertinent to this study in this light as their third person voices mingle with their own, first-person experience. They also represent three strands in the project of retrieving, and so returning women's voices and musicianship to the punk back catalogue and public debate. One approach, within feminist sensibilities, is Abigail Gardner who considers women in music, as individual acts and cultural agents, from the perspective of age studies. Hers is a research trajectory addressing how aging as part of women's life cycle tends to be either erased or framed in stereotypes around female aging. Gardner looks at what happens to female musicians as they get older, how they regard their own aging, and social attitudes to the 'older' woman, particularly in the youth-encoded pop music scene, performing on stage. There is much to be considered in this domain, and for research across those disciplinary areas that would consider such topics (women's health, sex-gender psychopathologies, performance studies, media and communications, music research for instance). The authors in this study certainly have something to say about their own shift in biological terms, from young woman, starting out DIY punk, to older, experienced creative, professional or returning artist: Viv Albertine and Patti Smith each write about returning to public performance after taking time out, to live their other lives, as does Black. When considering when, and why a female musician would consider writing her memoir Gardner takes aging as her analytical and political lens through which to evaluate the careers of women in music as they get older in line of her larger project to situate menopause in women's studies and those concentrating on aging.[45]

As noted in Chapter One, there are limitations to this, somewhat biologically reductionist, explanation of why a woman might write a memoir, and at what age, let alone at what age a female musician should consider her on-stage persona; an anxiety to which none of these women concede: Patti Smith through to Kim Gordon, and Pauline Black all have commented on aging in passing, not as an end point in their careers.[46] Memoir-writing is an activity that a writer embarks upon later in their adult life, whatever chronological age that might entail. This applies to *manopausal* male exponents of the memoir genre as well, music ones in particular. And as Greta Thunberg (b. 2003), who as a teenager spearheaded the School Strikes for the Climate and Extinction Rebellion movements, shows in her co-written memoir from 2020 one is never too young to publish a memoir even if collabo-written with older others. As Simone de Beauvoir and, more recently, Karl Ove Knausgård also show, a memoir can be as detailed, as lengthy, and as multiple as it can be as brief and diverse in its literary style, written during an author's lifetime, published posthumously, or as a publicity vehicle (as is the case, I would argue, for the Debbie Harry memoir). Beauvoir published multiple volumes on her life, times, lovers, published between 1958 and 1972, all densely detailed. In another vein, a hit in publishing and punditry terms, consider the aforementioned Karl Ove Knausgård (b. 1968) who has taken the self-authored male gaze into another level of public 'over-sharing' in his six 'autobiographical novels' entitled *My Struggle* (*Min Kamp* in Norwegian).

A second approach, written not so much as an academic research project but as a recollection of having been there, as a punk super-fan, music journalist and punk performer for a brief period, Vivian Goldman, provides another angle on punk times, personalities, and playlists that celebrate female contributions. Her celebratory book-cum-mixtape from 2019, *Revenge of the She-Punks: A Feminist Music History from Poly Styrene to Pussy Riot*, covers a number of recurring themes running through the lyrics of her selected playlists. This is an interesting, and fun approach that is premised on the main meaning, for performers, fans, and analysts, of punk politics being contained primarily in the lyrics. An approach that Viv Albertine also endorses, it is harder to maintain in the case of Cosey Fanni Tutti's experimental work with Throbbing Gristle and later electronica with Chris and Cosey which are mostly instrumentals. Goldman extrapolates some core insights about how 'she-punks' express their refusal to conform to the sanitized lyrical content of mainstream pop at the time, how their song titles and experiences evoked in the tracks also set an agenda for topics that male journalists and musicians would not broach: Alice Bag underscores the Goldman approach to punk music analysis in this regard when she considers some of the best known tracks of the Bags, while Nina Hagen considers the power of metaphor, intentional or perceived in her recollection of cultural censorship in former East Germany. The track is 'Du hast den Farbfilm vergessen' ('You forgot [to bring] the colour film') from 1974. In Hagen's cover version with her first band, it became a hit, construed as a satirical take on the monochromatic effects of East German censorship. This hit catapulted Hagen, 19 at the time, into the spotlight, confirming her own sense of destiny.[47] Most of the authors consider their lyric writing as core pursuit, even as they extol the power of guitar riffs (Smith Start), ensemble playing (Brownstein), production values and arranging prowess (Albertine writing about Ari Up in the studio), the countercultural, race and class inflections of beat, rhythm, and power chords (Bag, Black, and Gordon), and multiculturalism as a measure for band line-ups (a characteristic of 2-tone musicmaking and prominent in Black's musico-political commitments). Women were also writing about, expressing, and experiencing first-hand the punk tropes of anger, violence, and acoustics of 'noise'.

One female academic who can claim authority as headliner punk musician and scholar is Helen Reddington, known as Helen McCookerybook from the Chefs and then Helen and the Horns. As a scholar, Reddington has done much to recuperate the musicmaking of 'lost women' through interview-work with practitioners, still performing and those no longer, in a study that is also partial memoir. Like Goldman, Reddington's third person voice resonates with her own personal experience and networks as a 'she-punk' alongside her fieldwork and interview-based research findings. It underscores how nonsensical it is to claim that passion, personal experience (also known as autoethnography), and scholarly rigour cannot co-exist in academic research. At the time of publication, the still under construction, online edition of the *Oxford Handbook of Punk Rock* exemplifies this liminal space. The editors, George McKay and Gina Arnold, note alongside their academic credentials that they are a former punk and former writer for *Rolling Stone* magazine respectively. Gone are the days, in this corner of academe at least, when an academic felt the need to obscure other pursuits. In the case of punk music writing the hierarchy of legitimacy has effectively been flipped. Punk-ness has become an intellectual badge of honour, a figurative form of psychogeography through punk's back catalogue.

Figure 4: Nina Hagen
Artist: Mauricio Escobar (all rights reserved)

Figuring as colleagues, objects of desire and aspiration, and favourite punk acts in the memoir-set, the reader encounters women writing as (once) novice performers and now writing as novice writers, all except for Patti Smith who was already a noted poet before she went on stage to sing. They show themselves to be engaged observers of the geocultural and sexual politics of their time as they reveal their inner worlds as audiences and fans of other artists (male and female) across the music spectrum. Take for example odes to the work of earlier and contemporaneous musicians such as ; Janis Joplin, for Brix Smith Start, indirectly for Patti Smith but less so for Chrissie Hynde whose groupie attraction was for Iggy Pop; 'I'd been in love with this Class A piece of tail for my entire band life and before...'.[48] Cher provides Brix Smith Start with her 'first lesson in the art of power dressing' and whose love for Disneyland is an emotional leitmotiv throughout her book, part source of her own musical inspirations and part-portent of her eventual split from Mark E. Smith.[49] Kathleen Hanna from the American, riot grrrls signature band, Bikini Kill is for Carrie Brownstein one of her most formative influences. It is Patti Smith herself for Viv Albertine, Alice Bag and Nina Hagen; Chrissie Hynde for Brix Smith Start in turn. These role models straddle musical, and taste divides as well. For example, the polar opposite of punkish DIY-ness in musical and sartorial terms, Karen Carpenter (lead singer and drummer of the Carpenters), is a major star to whom Kim Gordon writes a fan letter, dedicates a song – 'Tunic' – and extols in her memoir.[50] At last it is OK for readers (me included I should add) to acknowledge the 'guilty pleasure' of liking the Carpenters, and Karen's singing (I also recall mourning her death, from anorexia nervosa, on hearing the news while browsing through the import bins of a record shop) now that Kim Gordon, and Viv Albertine 'fess up to being Karen Carpenter fans. With these admissions the "straightest" woman in pop becomes a punk's icon long after her tragic death.

The inclusion of non-punk artists is important to the complex cross-references at work within any single memoir, or cluster. In the case of the Carpenters sound and production values so not punk, Karen Tongson goes deeper into the Karen Carpenter *fangrrrl* phenomenon in her 2021 semi-autobiographical study entitled *Why Karen Carpenter Matters*. Tongson focuses on the race-sexuality axis of what it meant to be a Karen Carpenter fan, not only of Carpenter's extraordinary voice, drumming skills, and musicianship. Tongson's fascination positions Carpenter as an icon of (queer) transgressiveness despite Carpenter personifying the sort of mainstream and heteronormative studio pop that both punk rhetoric and feminist critiques of the music business push back against. At least this is the case for Tongson, named after Carpenter, an American Filipina musicologist, musician and daughter of established musicians from the Philippines who immigrated to the States.[51] Arthur Rimbaud, William Burroughs, Sam Shepard, Marc Bolan, along with other (popular) cultural figures such as Walt Disney, Gok Wan, Burt Bacharach, 'Nordic Noir' crime television, Vivienne Westwood, Nigel Kennedy (who became Brix Smith Start's husband after she left Mark E. Smith), Sun Ra, Marianne Faithfull, and – once again – Malcolm McLaren also make multiple entrances and exits, in various guises. The 'Sid and Nancy' story (Sid Vicious of the Sex Pistols and his ill-fated relationship with Nancy Spungen) features in the Chrissie Hynde and Viv Albertine memoirs from different points of view. In short, the amount of (mutual) cross-referencing is rich in their contemporaneous and retrospective affection, as continuity device but also as part of the texture of these reminiscences when seen as a larger body of work.

Being There: Memoirs as Primary Source

'[F]or the more I saw of the world, the more I realized that is was brimming over with all I could ever hope to experience, understand, and put into words.' (Simone de Beauvoir)[52]

'The racial identity that marks me out in society is worn beneath my skin every day. My father's colour envelops me and that is unconditional love of a kind, Indeed, one almost might say black by design.' (Pauline Black)[53]

Simone de Beauvoir (1908-1986) and Pauline Black exemplify, in the passages cited above, the ways in which a first-person narrative can work to reveal, as it also redacts the recollected interconnections between the personal and the political, a private and public life. One of the foremost French public intellectuals of post-World War Europe, a founder of existentialist philosophy, Beauvoir's investigations into the sociopolitical issues of her times includes her classic, proto-feminist treatise *The Second Sex* published in 1949 though not available for English-speaking readers until some years later. Beauvoir was also a novelist and playwright, a left-wing political activist of the day, and patron of socially engaged arts and public culture. In her writing, Beauvoir is well aware of what a memoir can or cannot offer a reader looking for revelatory truth. She considers memoirs as one sort of literary fiction, a form that provides her with a license to re-articulate autobiographical details on record to her selected personal recollections, all of which serve her wider existentialist and political project of philosophy, a lifelong commitment she shared with Jean-Paul Sartre. Preceding best-selling male memoirists like Karl Ove Knausgård by a substantial margin, Beauvoir's multi-volume memoirs set the bar for articulating a form of public introspection that merges the first person with the wider 'we' of 'you, me, and the rest of us'. She does this from a privileged, geocultural and gender-class standpoint that foregoes the need to displace her first person with a scholarly, third person voice.

Beauvoir is a pioneer in the authoritative female autobiographical voice as she recounts, in personal and philosophical terms, what she considers it takes to 'become' rather than be 'born a woman'.[54] Diverse schools of feminist, political and philosophical thought add their voices to this ongoing riddle in music research as well. Judith Peraino observes in debates about whether more recent schools of feminist research offer a viable political project for the next generation of feminist scholars and women's rights activists that 'the normative structures we call family and nation, gender, race, class, and sexual identity ... whatever looks like the inevitable' remain forces to be reckoned with.[55] Gender politics in light of women's rights activism and reappraisals of women's contribution to public culture are subtext, and explicit references for the memoirists and will be addressed accordingly in subsequent chapters. Patti Smith, whose prose resembles lyrical long-form poetry rather than detailed chronological reconstructions, comes close to Beauvoir's self-aware, crafted literary approach in, *Just Kids* (2010), *M Train* (2015), and *Year of the Monkey* (2017). Carrie Brownstein in her memoir, *Hunger Makes Me a Modern Girl* from 2015 also shows a style that resonates with both Beauvoir and Smith in their literary inflections.

Comments on style, such as those above, are hazardous. Suffice it to say that this digression from the punk-verse to Beauvoir, who wrote not a word on music as such, underscores how for women who have been public figures publishing a memoir is not a novel event. The 'rise of the female rock memoir'.[56] has been noticed as part of a trend in the arts and entertainment industry that includes the memoirs of female comedians. In both cases, getting on to best-seller lists has been seen as 'propelling their authors from acts to brands.'[57] As Hadley Freeman notes in her review of "bad girl" comedian Amy Shumer's, *The Girl with the Lower Back Tattoo*, the line between authenticity and branding is a fine one indeed: an unease that is echoed in responses to memoirs from women in music. Nonetheless, the question remains: 'how narrow the parameters still are for women in the public eye, who are expected to be exceptional but also an everywoman. ... [considered] a triumph of equality when a woman admits to enjoying sex?'[58] On that note, Cosey Fanni Tutti is the most candid, a musician for whom the sex industry become a medium for her own public performance art (more on this in Chapter Five). Completing this line of thought, one could also consider how it is also just as transgressive, even if disappointing for fans looking for extraordinariness, read prominent punk women writing about domesticity, 'ordinary' life, admitting to *not* enjoying sex – a sentiment that Viv Albertine discusses at some length in both her memoirs.

(Women) Writing about (Making) Music

> 'I'm going to remember everything and then I'm going to write it all down. An aria for a coat. A requiem for a café. That's what I was thinking, in my dream, looking down at my hands.' (Patti Smith)[59]

> 'When you sit down to think about your life, as I have had to for this book, you have to look back over some things you've kept out of the daylight of your mind for years, and they can catch you.... It's funny too how you don't have much control over what it is you do remember; how the most inconsequential, unimportant events sit in the front of your mind as clear as yesterday and the moments you just ache to relive stay out of reach for days or weeks a time.' (Nina Simone)[60]

In the first of the above citations, Patti Smith draws a stylistic and thematic line between *M Train*, her second memoir, and the chronological narrative of her first, *Just Kids*, that focuses on her relationship with the artist Robert Mapplethorpe in mid-twentieth century New York's underground cultural scene; a story 'that was obliged to wait until I found the right voice'.[61] This period is also when Smith moved from writing Rimbaud-inflected poetry, living with Mapplethorpe and sharing together the first steps in their respective artistic-literary paths (some reduce this relationship to Smith as Mapplethorpe's muse) to acting, writing plays, and then incorporating piano and guitar into the sung-recited performances that were to establish her as musician-poet. The passage cited above is at the end of the penultimate chapter of *M Train*[62] as she addresses the reader directly (echoes of Charlotte Bronte's ending to *Jane Eyre* here). It leads out one of her most moving paragraphs; on loss, time passing (shades here of Marcel Proust as reviewers note) as Smith evokes the image of her sitting down 'to open my notebook. And begin to write something new.'[63]

The second quote is from Nina Simone's autobiography, written with Stephen Cleary. Whilst outside the generation, racial divide, and musical genre of most memoirists here, this passage articulates the psycho-emotional resonances to remembering-with-intent, the curiosities of memory and forms of recollection as sources for narrative – and analysis. How much detail is enough? Where to draw the line between over-sharing, and candid revelation? How to write about others who are still alive, with whom relationships have been both positive, fraught, or destructive in one's life out of respect or, perhaps, the need to avoid litigation? How to cross-check one's memories with the official, personal, and community historical records?

For women who have carved out a career as musicians, from jazz through to the blues, punk, and other sorts of stadium-rock stardom, another figurative modality of authorial *voice* plays a role; the putative authenticity of the first-hand account of an artist's life and work effectively reverses the reviewer-pundit mirror back on itself. Such issues concern the memoirist as well as the researcher as both draw on a range of sources, personal and public, to weave this version of stories often told by others. Should we take these memoirs as more truthful, more legitimate than the rich literature of (feminist and trade) biographies of women in music? In comprehensive literature reviews the emphasis is on what sort of contribution a precursor spate of biographies of women in music can make to the historical record of western popular and classical art music, from a feminist perspective:[64] for instance, work that retrieves female musicians from erasure or disinterest; work looking to move beyond the cliché of women in music being primarily about the lives, and deaths of tragic female music stars; Amy Winehouse (1983-2011) being one of the most recent, Janis Joplin (1943-1970) and Billie Holiday (1915-1959) from further back in the annals of Western, that is Anglo-American popular music and its discontents.

One bone of contention between successive generations of feminist research and activism, *Second Wave* to *Third Wave* so-called, is how to reconcile the public personae of high-profile women artists, still in the minority, and their cultural legacy and do so without reducing, or even inflating their own accounts to discussions about the sex-gender stereotyping of women in public life; by supporters and denigrators alike. The case of Madonna, whose impact on popular culture, women in pop music and LGBTQ communities in the 1980s has become an academic research domain. Madonna's legacy, together with those of Lady Gaga, Rihanna, and Beyoncé more recently, see scholars and pundits struggling with where their agency, control over their creative output and public image, begins and where control by the sexploitative tendencies of the global music industry ends. For Black artists, and other women of colour whose work is integral to rap and hip-hip culture, also predominantly masculinist, debates about sexual agency, propriety over some artists' performative embodiments are fraught with racialized as well as gendered biological essentialist tropes. How to study these phenomenal acts in ways that unpack rather than perpetuate stereotypes of women as exceptional, larger than life high achievers? Is ordinariness an acceptable characteristic when relating a life off stage?

All these issues are grist to the mill of music researchers interested in taking women's stories, their back catalogues, and role in shaping music making across the spectrum seriously. However, rumbling between the lines of trade press attention to music (auto)biographies, is how women musicians' memoirs square up to the sales figures and reviewers' thumbs-up for those from male artists; those from Bob Dylan and Keith Richards (of the Rolling Stones) in particular. To illustrate, Rob Sheffield, in *Rolling Stone* magazine rates Smith's *Just Kids* as second to Bob Dylan, just ahead of Keith Richards in his league table of the '25 Greatest Rock Memoirs of all Time' from 2012 and eight years later in an expanded update.[65] Out of the 2012 list only three memoirs were by women (Patti Smith, Kristin Hersh, and Ronnie Spector), with five Black artists only on this list (including Ronnie Spector). By 2020, Sheffield was able to include some of the authors studied here: Smith retained her runner-up spot to Dylan's no. 1, Albertine made it to No. 6, Brownstein to No. 10, (Ronnie Spector is at no. 14, Kristin Hersh from the Throwing Muses at no. 21), Gordon makes it at the half-way point at no. 25, (Tegan and Sara at no. 38), Debbie Harry enters at no. 46, ahead of Alice Bag at no. 48. With more women in the music business publishing memoirs, this pundit who notes that 'great rock memoirs don't always come from great artists' has been able to improve his gender-balance rating somewhat over the years; from five to ten female authors, and with now ten artists from African-American, Latinx, or First Nation backgrounds, still only a fifth to two-fifths of the acts named in this 'Top Fifty'. The majority of publications remain those from white, male musicians: Danyel Smith in her chronicle of Black women in American pop music is clear about the 'white-washing' that underscores such unconscious bias.[66] Chrissie Hynde, who worked as a music journalist for *New Musical Express* in her early years in the UK is clear about the negative influence of trade publications in this regard; 'I was as frustrated as the rest of them – a frustrated musician (the cliché of music journalism), opinionated, hungover, illegal in the workplace, devoid of ambition and if I couldn't find a word in my dumb guy vocabulary I would make one up. ... The more dismissive and poorly written my reviews, the more the NME applauded me. ...They liked it bad and that was good.'[67] Brownstein reserves some of her most acerbic writing to the sexist ways in which the music press covered Sleater-Kinney, complete with examples of some of the worst offenders in her eyes.[68] Albertine also attests to the entrenched prejudice of the music press during the Slits heyday, abuse and gratuitous violence from passers-by on the street, or during hostile gigs.

Nina Simone's memoir, a precursor to how Alice Bag and Pauline Black articulate their experience performing in public, is a reminder of the under-articulated race-gender dimensions to how artists get recording contracts, gigs, and wider recognition over time. Most of the memoirists here do not actively engage this dynamic though. Viv Albertine is particularly reserved about the formative role that Afro-Caribbean music (dub and reggae) played in the Slits repertoire and signature sound, exemplified in their breakthrough album, *Cut*. These rhythms and production values played no small part in generating the band's sound at the outer edges of the thrashing, three-chord, three-minute punk songs of the time. It also somewhat underplays the ground-breaking roles that British producers and musicians of Afro-Caribbean heritage such as Dennis Bovell (b. 1953) played in producing *Cut*, or Don Letts (b. 1956) who directed the Slits' first videos and who also worked with Chrissie Hynde.

Predictably, the exceptions to such ellipses come from authors who are women of colour, Alice Bag and Pauline Black. Alice Bag echoes Nina Simone's memoir which opens with a chapter about Simone's hometown, her Indian and African slave descendants, and her childhood in the segregated south despite the 'very cordial' relations Simone as a child experienced between the black and white communities.[69] In her memoir opening Bag portrays her childhood growing up in Los Angeles in a poor, Mexican community, speaking only Spanish until that was knocked out of her in school. For her part, Pauline Black writes eloquently about the racial tensions in the same period, growing up as a mixed-race adopted child in a provincial city in the UK. Chrissie Hynde's noting of the musical racial divide in her account of growing up in the American mid-West notwithstanding, most of the authors do not reflect on their relatively privileged position as white performers in an industry divided along racial as well as gender lines, even as they take care to self-identify their family origins as working-class north London (Albertine) and Hull (Cosey Fanni Tutti), working-class New Jersey (Smith), middle-class mid-west and northwest US (Hynde and Brownstein), and well-off/middle class west coast US (Gordon, Smith Start).

Being a 'girl in a band' is ostensibly the key marker of counter-belonging as distinctiveness in a period in which punk claimed to change the name of the game.

Figure 5: Alice Bag,
Artist: Mauricio Escobar (all rights reserved)

The Memoirs: 'Dear Reader'

'Oh how I loved guys in bands. When a band played, time stood still.'
(Chrissie Hynde)[70]

'Being a woman and playing bass guitar, or any guitar, seemed about the coolest thing in the world to me. Too bad I couldn't really play. I didn't realize that it didn't matter. Punk had changed all of that. In less than a year I'd be writing my own songs, and playing in my own band. In three year's time I would be in England recording the first song I'd ever written. I'd be playing guitar and singing a duet on an album for The Fall.' (Brix Smith Start)[71]

Let's draw some observations about the memoirs, as a cluster of publications: The key device for shaping and organizing the timeline material is the artistic output, here mainly albums, songs, and in the case of Patti Smith, her poems and personal iconography of polaroid photos: a substantive aesthetic to all the short books that make up her memoir collection. Authors provide valuable insights about the labour, emotional if not spiritually significant processes involved in writing and performing music as part of a collective, of a movement that included variously articulated political allegiances, whether explicitly feminist, or not; as is the case with Albertine, Hagen, and Cosey.

Technical distinctions between a memoir and an autobiography aside, responses to the emerging body of punk rock *femoirs* have been mixed from academic and media commentators. As noted earlier in the case of female comedians' memoirs, there is an ongoing, almost neurotic concern expressed about whether such books from female celebrities are bona fide: no such reservations for those by male musicians. For academics, Abigail Gardner exemplifies this unease with her representation of female musician-memoirizing as a genus of the self-confessional. In Gardner's view the first personhood of these accounts underscores the mythology of 'neoliberal individualism' in publications categorized as 'triumph over diversity' narratives.[72] Some circumspection has its place when approaching any cultural artefact that has a large corporate marketing machine behind it (publishers and recording companies alike). Indeed, punk's most iconic act, the Sex Pistols and their in-your-face manager Malcolm McLaren encapsulate this ambivalence. In their heyday and since, the Sex Pistols have been continually framed as nothing much more than a branding vehicle for McLaren's self-aggrandising agenda, thereby eschewing serious engagement with their musical output, a substantial contribution to punk musicalities. It also overlooks how McLaren's reputation runs along the well-worn continuum of self-regarding rock 'n' roll manager. These sorts of authentication concerns about female music-memoirists tend to erase the authorial voice and agency of authors who are, after all, recounting their own, direct experience of 'sexploitation' in the music world, including punkish anti-establishment versions thereof.

The issue with the condemnation of any creative act as the product of 'neoliberal individualism', or 'branding' to use the current terminology, is that, in one fell swoop, all agency, all of the creative complexity, all the references to shared and specific experiences (of abuse, violence, joy, ecstasy, spirituality – you name it) that pulsate in the manifest content, as well as between the lines, are effaced. Reductionist assessments do not do justice to how any memoir is selective, full of 'holes', a curated artefact; borne out by the disappointment many Beauvoir admirers experienced, and I am one, when learning of details in her published correspondence with Jean-Paul Sartre that counter the serenity of her own accounts of her intimate relationships, with Sartre and others. The tendency to focus on the singular, larger than life personalities who may be part of such accounts does not do service to these from female punk exponents given the numerous references to teamwork, creative collaboration, working and living together that provide the bulk of the accounts. The awareness and commitment to the DIY ethos of creative communalism, articulated in the findings of Reddington's study and echoed in Goldman, balance out episodes of survival, suffering – personal and professional – of making and performing counter-cultural music against the odds.

Style, Form, Substance

This section runs though some of these shared and individual features as these resonate with analysis of some of the music discussed in the books. First, there are crossovers in the way the books are organized, narrative overlaps and distinctive characteristics of literary style and attention to chronological details for instance, discernible when considering them together as each author took to her screen, notebook, or was commissioned to write her memoirs over the last decade or so. The memoir of Kathleen Hanna, from Bikini Kill, who is considered as the epitome of the 1990s riot grrrl phenomenon, has finally made it to press. The early deaths, from cancer, of Ari Up (the Slits) and Poly Styrene (X-Ray Spex), put paid to any chance of their writing their own stories: now being reconstructed by others in film, or references in other publications: Nina Hagen and Viv Albertine talk a lot about their relationship with Ari Up, as friend and bandmate respectively.

Most of the books, a life-story with early years and up to time of writing, follow usual timeline chronologies; Patti Smith is the exception as she distributes her chronology over separate episodes in shorter volumes, playing with surrealist recollections from her working life, and her dreamlife. Several start with variously entitled prologues (Smith, Brownstein, Albertine, and Hynde), others include epilogues that consciously address the reader. Kim Gordon's *Girl in a Band* is the exception in this case and also for not providing a Table of Contents. With or without such a table (two separate ones for Viv Albertine's memoirs in two parts), the chapter titles can be read as both chronologies and play-lists that start at the end (Gordon, Smith) or somewhere in the middle of dream-worlds (Smith, Smith Start), biographical and creative timelines in a variety of chronological and thematic ordering; for example, Brownstein organizes her memoir in three parts; 'Youth', 'Sleater-Kinney' and 'Aftermath', Hynde opens with her earliest memory, as do Brix Smith Start, Nina Hagen, Pauline Black, Chrissie Hynde, and Cosey Fanni Tutti. Parents and primary caregivers, private and more public genealogies, are presented in various measures of detail. Patti Smith is the most oblique in how she brings in those close to her, many of whom have passed away; Robert Mapplethorpe in the first book, along with Fred Smith in the second. Sam Shepard, and Sandy Pearlman whose death she mourns, feature in *Year of the Monkey*. One's family tree, however (re)constructed matters for all the authors though in differing proportions and timelines along the aforementioned class-gender-race axes, made explicit or not. In the case of Nina Hagen (whose mother made her career as an East-German movie star, her birth father and later stepfather non-conformists, public political dissidents), her familial and cultural genealogy informs her own sense of self and creative destiny (her words) growing up in the once divided Germany.

Organizational decisions, chapter titles and order, indicate care in the selection of memory and shaping of a particular narrative arc between introspection and confessional through the various lenses of explicit political or countercultural persuasions. The inclusion of photos, artwork, and facsimiles of personal correspondence are common to all, though are more than branding add-ons or the obligatory photographic archives in the case of Patti Smith's curation of her own polaroid still-lives; an aesthetic practice she has continued to develop. As is the case with public figures and this literary genre, all include various levels of caveat emptor with explicit, and no doubt coded messages in their respective acknowledgement sections. In terms of style and tense, some use direct quotes from diary entries, Albertine in particular. She also includes asides to the reader in italics, meta-comments at-time-of-writing as another way of providing multiple voices from times-past into the present narrative; the voice of young Viv and her mates as pop/punk music devotees and 'dedicated followers of fashion' narrates Part One in *Clothes, Clothes, Clothes, Music, Music, Music, Boys, Boys, Boys* – feel the rhythm in the title. Part Two of this, her first memoir belongs, in part, to the "desperate housewife" then cancer survivor and rehabilitated artist and performer of more recent years. In *Reckless*, the present-tense voice of the young, 'reckless' and drug-addict Chrissie Hynde merges into that of her older – clean – self. The point here is that none of these books rely on the single narrative voice-over or linear chronology. They all look to mix tense, voice, and with that perspective on past events retold within the formalities of a lifetime, relationship or creative arc: beginnings are endings; endings are positioned as returns – of bands, relationships, families, educations, health, creativity, lust for life.

Sex, Drugs, and Rock 'n' Roll

> 'And in the end this story is a story of drug abuse.' (Chrissie Hynde)[73]

Authors broach the topic of sex, and sexuality in a range of ways that go well beyond accounts of sexual violence and abuse. For instance, Albertine makes a point of her own in her first chapter 'Masturbation', Brownstein is the only author to depict, discretely, her relationships with women including her closest musical collaborator, Corin Tucker, as well as her father's struggles with his own homosexuality. *Just Kids*, Patti Smith's memoir of her early career and life with Robert Mapplethorpe does address his emerging homosexuality, and the link between his art and interest in sadomasochism. *M Train* and *Year of the Monkey* are more distanced, dreamlike in their voicing of what are effectively requiems. Smith does not dwell on intimacies, bar an occasional reference to her late husband, Frank 'Sonic' Smith or recollections of her relationship with playwright and actor Sam Shepard (1947-2017) in *Year of the Monkey*, who she supported in completing his final writing as his death approached. Kim Gordon's memoirs are framed by the break-up of her marriage with Thorston Moore (b. 1958), co-founder of Sonic

Youth; ending her book with how on retreating from a sexual encounter with 'a player, I knew full well' she realises that she has become 'someone else entirely.'[74] Smith Start and Hynde provide more classical, rock stars-behaving-badly stories including those darker episodes (the material that reviewers and PR machines tend to feed off) such as rape, physical violence, depression, substance abuse and, in the case of Albertine and Cosey Fanni Tutti, serious illness and recovery.

Each author devises her own path around the expectation that such a memoir will, in the time-honoured tradition have (fe)male (punk) rock stars behaving badly, being sexually precocious as the focal point of their narrative. Each author deals with the presumption that there will be details on the intimate, sex and love lives of various protagonists in their own way; in cases names are suppressed while others are already public record. In terms of more personal levels, Albertine is one of the most explicit and relentless in her detailing of bodily functions and desires, setting up and then batting away this very expectation. Patti Smith, on the other hand, relies on allusion and ellipsis while Cosey Fanni Tutti, Hagen, Hynde, and Smith Start all consider their own memories less front-on. Cosey is clear about her alternative lifestyle living with and sharing beds with her Throbbing Gristle comrades though less revealing in many ways about her inner emotional life. Pauline Black is more candid in some respects on this count. Carrie Brownstein broaches queer sexuality as she reflects on her upbringing with a difficult father and early years living and performing with Sleater Kinney's other frontwoman, Corin Tucker. Kim Gordon, Brix Smith Start, Alice Bag, and Viv Albertine probe into their own body-image, struggles with how others perceived them, on stage and in their families, while Pauline Black, along with Alice Bag, puts racialized embodiment and the combined sexism-racism they encountered from audiences and industry actors squarely onto their autobiographical agenda.

Collaborative DIY as Leadership

But it is collaboration that is the strongest theme in these accounts, as well as a key organizational device for linking the personal to the political, and both to the musical in the respective narratives. Artistic endeavour and achievements, disappointments and dud albums included are not solitary processes. They are part of significant if not lifelong periods of working together. Whether this is specific to womanhood or not, the demands of a music industry and music press looking for heroes, villains and fallen stars is a constant pressure on keeping the collaborative, social dimensions to music-making to the fore. Creative and professional relationships constitute the lion's share of up to several thousands of pages of musical life. This means discussing the (mostly male) egos of their collaborators and managements. This is integral to Brix Smith Start's account of her time with the Fall, married, and then divorced life with Mark E. Smith, the band's notoriously autocratic leader and creative impulse. Writing credits, presence (audible) in the final mix; where to stand on stage, how to cope with infidelity, and the practicalities of life on the road for a woman, or as the female spouse ('what happens on the bus, stays on the bus') all require constant negotiation.

We see here not so much treatises on the gender politics of sex, drugs, and rock 'n' roll but thick descriptions of the everyday life, the slog of making music, performing, and recording in unconventional, uncompromising ways; a prevalent theme in Albertine's portrayal of Ari Up in the studio. There is in this regard little glamour to these gritty, in some cases gritted-teeth accounts. Brix Smith Start is particularly explicit about these internal tensions in *The Rise, The Fall, and The Rise*, as these are germane to the Fall timeline and its hefty back catalogue and band member changes, forty years long until Mark E. Smith's death in 2018. Part two of the book is all about the Fall and in this regard can be taken as a conscious corrective to both audience and music press perceptions of her contribution to the band's output: 'The Fall was an autocracy, with Mark as the dictator. When it began in the 1970s it was very much a collective but [by the time she joined] the last remnants of democracy were gone. It was Mark's band'.[75] There is a lot more to discuss here. Suffice it to say, any Fall fan can remember the music press's disparaging treatment of Brix's arrival and supposed negative influence. She notes how these criticisms of creeping commercialism undermined her creative contribution at the same time as she admits her desire for the band to have more commercial success. Smith Start has gone on to found and front other bands, including Brix and the Extricated with former members of the Fall.

And here is Chrissie Hynde, ending her memoir with a eulogy to her deceased collaborators, underscoring the formative influence key members of the Pretenders had on her musical development and emotional life, guitarist, James (Jimmy) Honeyman-Scott in particular. She writes, 'Jimmy would transform my songs in a way I could only have hoped for in my wildest imaginings'.[76] The predominant tone therefore is about music-making as process, an approach that Christopher Small articulated in his landmark study.[77] Making music is happening communally and as self-identified punkish communities (e.g. 2-tone/indie/riot grrrl), as a socially engaged and creative undertaking that requires the necessary labour of writing, rehearsing, of making collaborative work "work." Here is Hynde again: 'I loved taking my songs to the band and having them transformed. I knew I loved singing but it took me a long time to feel like I owned it.... The feeling of being at home overrode the rest, and that feeling came with a guitar slung over my shoulder while standing in front of a microphone. Home at last.'[78]

When personal relationships start to change, go sour or disintegrate, how to maintain a professional approach to performing and recording becomes an end in itself, as Albertine, Smith Start, Gordon, Bag, and Cosey attest to each in their own way. For anyone looking to find "dirt" on the deficiencies of famous friends and acquaintances, or resentments towards other band-members and collaborators there is relatively little to find; Cosey is the most up-front about ongoing struggles in this regard. There are, nonetheless, plenty of dry, witty and well-written accounts of conflicts, along with variously enjoyed sexual, and platonic encounters with other key figures such as Iggy Pop, Johnny Rotten, Sid Vicious, Courtney Love, inter alia. Read and smile. That said, the generosity in giving credit where credit is due (perhaps more than need be for in the case of Smith Start she remains loyal to Mark E. Smith's creative intuition despite his many excesses – drug and alcohol induced, and sexual infidelities) is not sentiment. We see also enough moments where the authors talk about the sexual politics of misappropriations and erasures by pundits. Hynde is particularly clear about this occupational hazard, the consequences of 'giving credit away' with respect to androcentric reporting in the trade press;[79] an issue mentioned in passing by others such as Albertine, Gordon, Smith Start and Cosey as they (re)construct the authorship tensions for tracks, album credits, and less literal musical developments in which they played a significant role, only to see public kudos, and copyright earnings accrue to their male colleagues.

Outro: Punk as Art

The tension, in the literature as well as in public and political debates, between art on the one hand and politics on the other is particularly acute in the case of punk music as a political intervention, popular culture, and artform. Perhaps because the first wave of punk musicians positioned themselves through an anti-establishment aesthetics, in terms of their visuals (unkempt, non-fashionable, not glam-rock) and audible presence (loud, seemingly unrehearsed, out of time, off-key, lo-fi production values, confrontational) this notion that punk music making is also an art form seems like an oxymoron. Contending ways of thinking about this tension point to conflicting presumptions about what "art" means, particularly sonic – musical – formats, when considered next to those debates about the nature and purpose of "politics." At least in the early days, punk by its very self-representation mounted a visceral sonic and visual challenge to elitist pop music cultures and, by association, highbrow musico-political pretensions.

3. FINDING VOICE

Intro

> 'punk rock, [is a] genre of music [that is] so menacing and physically savage...' (Talk Show Host)[80]

The above characterization of punk music as *menacing* is taken from an American TV talk show in 1977 (mentioned in Chapter Two) featuring Iggy Pop, whose confrontational attitude towards his host echoed that of the Sex Pistols' behaviour in their infamous appearance on a British TV show the previous year. Epithets like 'physically savage' evoke the masculinity of on-stage performance and off-stage public persona that has become the hallmark of punk's cultural legacy whatever high-profile artists might have represented for political activism of their day. Women excelling in said "physical savagery" was and continues to be an exception.

The next chapters pivot on a cluster of themes threaded through the books, including a selection of tracks, some discussed in the memoirs and some not. In this chapter I look at the theme of *voice*, *guitar* is the theme for Chapter Four, and the *not-strictly-musical* dimensions to creative working lives is the theme for Chapter Five. The rubrics emerge out of my own multiple readings of accumulated (cross) references to the first two themes. The third is a means to update and extrapolate from beyond the published narratives as their protagonists continue to create, perform, and explore new creative avenues, including reuniting as has been the case for Sleater-Kinney and the Selecter. This curatorial device is one way to navigate the many, diverse recollections and overlaps within each memoir, between those penned by the one author (Smith, Albertine, and Bag for instance) and between authors who shared time with each other on stage, back stage, and as contemporaries once pictured together and now circulating as social media images in the online punk collective imaginary. After considering the analytical implications of *voice*, literally and figuratively speaking, when applied to female punk musicmaking by way of Roland Barthe's thinking on the relationship between music and society, I consider the qualities of the vocals of those memoirists whose voicings have been a formative element in the punk sonic repertoire.

Close listening of selected tracks, or samples, is juxtaposed to the authors' recollections, for the benefit of a first-time and familiar listener.[81]

Into the *Voice*

'There was no clearly defined punk sound, no dress code; all you had to do was show up and make your presence known. The movement was one of individuals and individual expression, each of us bringing our heritage and formative experiences with us in an organic and, in my case, unplanned way.' (Alice Bag)[82]

'I liked that I could buy some cool clothes, new boots and a good guitar.... I know I loved singing, but it took me a long time to feel like I owned it.' (Chrissie Hynde)[83]

Recollections from Alice Bag and Chrissie Hynde encapsulate the thrill and sense of (self) discovery offered to novice musicians realizing that, in the early years at least, getting to perform in public in a band was not down to having a manager, waiting to be discovered, or being able to play according to the conventions of pop musicianship of guitar-hero/keyboard or synthesizer virtuoso: 'all we needed was the guts to try'.[84] The authoritative, I-was-there voice is evident in these two passages. But there is more to consider in the case of women punk musicians, in their own words and how they sound, how others hear their musicmaking.

So, what am I getting at here when referring to *voice* in the context of the sex-gender politics of punk vocals? Here the voice – singing, murmured, semi-spoken – is a palpable entity, voice in its audible, sonic dimensions. This is distinct from *voice* in figurative terms; e.g. to consider authorship, the creative subject, sex-gender power hierarchies as these pertain to airplay and speaking rights (for women in particular) in public spaces. The second dimension is at play in what a reader can take as politically or culturally significant about memoirs from female artists. But the first, sonic as in the musical and not-strictly-musicalized qualities of voice, is the primary focus. The selected tracks and recollections from the memoir-set look at how artists found and then honed their vocal repertoire, as an audible challenge to the status quo based on stereotypes of female vocals being tuneful, on an aesthetics of sonic beauty that pleases, soothes.[85] In mainstream pop, male vocal lines tend to favour tenors, at the higher male vocal register, an aspect to the race inflections for considering African American female vocal registers, a point that Danyel Smith underscores in her 2022 study, *Shine Bright: A Very Personal History of Black Women in Pop*.

But is not just because as females, women in punk bands taking the vocal lead challenged the dominance of male timbres. The sonic disruption is also because the way women were singing, using their voice in and out of song, melodic but also anti-melodic, in tune but also not in tune provided the signature *timbre* and *texture* of punk vocal performance. This goes beyond noting that often times they were 'yelling', 'screaming', 'snarling' or 'growling'. They were also deploying spoken-sung techniques, known in the classical music vocal repertoire as *Sprechstimme*, or *Sprechgesang* in the German language conceptualisations.[86] Voice as "rough." loud and emphatic, provides the particular vocal pitches, volume, and vibrations onstage and in the studio that comprises punk's sonic challenge to the melodious status quo of the mainstream pop music industry. Male punk vocalists also excelled in these out-of-tune, off-key excesses; take, for instance, the joyful, subversive voice from how Sid Vicious (b. John Ritchie 1957-1979), bassist for the Sex Pistols (and whose life and death is somewhat of a leitmotiv in several memoirs),[87] covers the crooner evergreen, 'My Way'.

Several conceptual points arise here if we are to get past simplistic descriptors or reductionist notions of male vs. female vocal performance. The figurative sense of voice hereby joins the discussion, but only briefly given the extensive literature in philosophy, social and political theory, and feminism on these matters: First, recall how the women's movement from the 1960s -1970s sought to bring women as-a-group, and their missing, silenced voices into public spaces and political processes, a move matched in academic terms by projects to restore, retrieve, and highlight individual women's lives in empirical, and theoretical terms on the one hand and, on the other, incorporate the more inclusive, less biologically defined term *gender* in ways that go beyond its use as a synonym for women-as-a-group (see Chapter 2). A landmark study in this regard from the social sciences is Carol Gilligan's *In Another Voice*, published in 1982, on its 35th edition and still counting. *In Another Voice* presents Gilligan's riposte to mainstream behavioural psychological research into whether there is a measurable life-path of *moral development* along which an individual develops an understanding of what is the 'right' and what is the 'wrong' thing to do; a model of moral development in modern (read: liberal western) societies that proceeds from childhood to adulthood.

Taking a countermanding approach to published research into these questions, headed up by her mentor, Lawrence Kohlberg, Gilligan argues that any empirical research based on one, single demographic group let alone standardized questionnaires on how people respond to the open-endedness of any ethical dilemma leads to over-generalizations, more so when the research subjects are predominantly young, male university students.[88] Gilligan challenged these design elements in the Kohlberg study, included older women in her sample and gathered responses from qualitative, open-ended interviews. Written as Second Wave feminism was becoming an academic pursuit, the Gilligan study of how female respondents considered the same ethical dilemmas that were presented to male respondents in the initial study was ground-breaking. For all its own, liberal US-based tendencies to generalise about *Every Woman* that overlooks the intersections of other variables such as race, class, ethnicity, or religion, Gilligan's key finding was that female participants perceived right and wrong, articulated their notion of so-called moral reasoning, quite differently to their male counterparts.

For Gilligan the final analysis is that, on the whole, men and women speak in *different voices*; distinct lifepaths and experiences form how a person thinks about right and wrong, social responsibility which, in the case of the women in Gilligan's study, pivot on an 'ethics of care' rather than on logical reasoning.[89] Gilligan concludes that androcentric research designs, exemplified by the Kohlberg experiment, reproduce the male-centred social structure, referred to as *patriarchy* in feminist scholarship of that era, in which women's voices are missing, and their life paths and utterances considered inferior to those of male subjects who (apparently, as this too is a presumption) reason according to 'rational-choice' utilitarian models of moral reasoning that Kohlberg and his fans favoured: The most prominent advocate for Kohlberg's theoretical model, of the male experience of "growing up" basically, at the time was the German philosopher Jürgen Habermas, who published on Kohlberg's paradigm as a model for the Good Society, even positing an additional – higher – stage of development. Very not-punk needless to say. Gilligan's findings still resonate with women reading her work for the first time, and decades later, as her findings underscore the feminist adage that research – like the personal, like making music – is also political.

A second dimension to consider is the aforementioned figurative notion of *voice* from mid-twentieth century critical schools of social and cultural theory; ways of thinking about the interrelationship between the arts, culture, and society that are quite different to the hypothesis-testing empiricism of Anglo-American behavioural psychology. A major thinker in this generation is the French semiologist (a scholar of *signs*, such as photography, music, cinema) Roland Barthes, in a collection of essays published in 1977 under the title of *Image – Music – Text*. For Barthes *voice* is not an abstract, theoretical idea or empirical, measurable entity but a social practice that includes the body, which is crucial to the dynamics of the relationship between an artist – or work of art, audience, and critics. In the essay, 'The Grain of the Voice', published in 1972, Barthes has this to say about why *voice* matters: it matters because the '"grain" of the voice is not – or is not merely – its timbre; the *significance* it opens cannot better be defined, indeed, than by the very friction between the music and something else.'[90] What Barthes means this 'something else' to be is beyond the scope of this discussion. Suffice it to say that for Barthes, the 'grain of the voice', the art and the part that communicates, is not just the sum of performance techniques; as he observes through the (less than flattering) case of the superstar, German classical singer Dietrich Fischer-Dieskau (1925-2012). It is not about beautiful diction or perfectly executed melodies, Barthes argues; 'nothing seduces' despite 'FD' being 'an artist beyond reproach.'[91]

In his critique of conventional aesthetics which lauds classical vocal virtuosity in western music making, namely where diction (ending consonants with greater emphasis than is usual in spoken-word) and accurate pitch are the goal, Barthes is effectively pointing to the power of the punk vocal, exemplified by Patti Smith and, I would add, Nina Hagen. In Barthes' view, perfect breath control of the singing voice, or articulation of word-endings – the consonants that do not serve as 'the springboard for the admirable vowels' do not necessarily provide listening pleasure.[92] Given that many vocal effects happen on the vowel sounds (across languages and music traditions), and that regional accents become audible through vowels rather than consonants it is not too big a leap to link Barthes' irreverent critique of the doyen of German lyric classical singing (Fischer-Dieskau) to a consideration of punk vocals in this case.[93] For it is the vowels that distinguish Patti Smith's vocals in many respects; the rhythmic, polemical push -and-pull between vowel, consonant, and syllable as well, and also a feature of Hagen's vocals. Barthes' consideration of what makes a vocal "work." in psycho-emotional terms, albeit from a classical art music perspective, provides a way to open our ears up to punk as polysemic, a complex sonics rather than mono-syllabic thrash as it is often characterized; in Barthes' words, the "grain" is that: 'the materiality of the body speaking its mother tongue.'[94]

Third, let's consider how the notion of voice merges with formal, techno-musicological considerations; punk, in live performance and in the studio.[95] All the authors consider how they discovered they could sing, or at least perform vocals that complemented the rough-and-ready instrumentals of their fledgling bands. Hagen, as a more operatically endowed and trained voice, dulled the edges of this classicist perfectionism with a range of techniques, tonal range and volume control. Patti Smith discovered and then cultivated a singing voice that comes close to that of Hagen. Ari Up, the Slits' lead vocalist, did nothing of the sort, refusing to melodize in ways that are inseparable from the Slits' sonic timbres and cadences (with a clear nod to Nina Hagen's ability to leap from low to high tones) to a reggae, rather than a rocky 4/4 beat. Brix Smith Start for her part was a female singing voice arriving in a formation led, irrevocably, by the snarl of Mark E. Smith's Mancunian-accented monologues, slurred consonants and northern working class vowels included. Singing, as such, in the early days of punk as a counter-musical movement was not sought after, whereas pushing back against the *bel canto* of global superstar vocalists such as Karen Carpenter or Joni Mitchell was, despite much admiration in retrospect (see Chapter Two). Alice Bag also began as a so-called screamer, the 'violence girl' persona she developed on stage sounded through her vocal delivery, also masking (if that is the right term) a natural singing voice that is evident in her later solo albums. Pauline Black talks more of rhythm, the visuals of being the front woman (of colour) as part of the ska-reggae dimensions of the 2-tone sound. For Black, as part of her career in theatre, a 'different voice' is conjoined with being a mixed-race performer in a cultural and national context dominated by the mellifluous received pronunciation of Royal Academy of Dramatic Art (RADA) graduates who are predominantly white, middle- and upper-class. *Voice* here denotes regional accents, class background, and race where the latter is distinguished by the accents of the West-Indies, Jamaica in particular, if not Africa; Black's biological father was, as she discovered later in life, Nigerian.

Punking up the Pop Rock Canon

Considering the qualities and role of punk-as-voice *in toto* also implies the voice of an instrument played against-the-grain or carried, personified in ways that directly defy the heteronormative and virtuoso performativity of 'cock rock', a term coined by Angela McRobbie and Simon Frith in their consideration of the sex-gender dimensions of rock guitar heroes of the 1970s.[96] Nearly fifty years apart, two scholars draw comparable allusions, albeit from different corners of academic and generations of inquiry, David Pearson and Roland Barthes:

> 'Similar to the way guitar chords in punk are about timbre more than harmony, punk vocals are about timbre and emotional intensity over pitch and melody.'[97]

> 'The "grain" is the body in the voice as it sings, the hand as it writes, the limb as it performs.'[98]

To recall, acts (self)-designated as punk are deconstructing the professionalised production values of mainstream pop rather than the formal, structural features of the so-called classical pop song. Neither are all the authors signed-up anti-capitalists, let alone feminists (more on such lines of demarcation in due course). It would be safe to assert that most bands in punk's first wave (1970s) revelled in their antipathy towards the music establishment, record companies and concert promotors, which opened up live performance and studio recording for newcomers, and women in particular. That was the point in the public rhetoric and demeanour of all the artist-memoirists featured here: "If they can do it, so can I" being the primary motivation to pick up a guitar, perform in public even when un(der)rehearsed, evocatively recalled by Alice Bag and Viv Albertine as they set out to be in a band, in East Los Angeles and North London respectively.

Not just reducible to respective levels of (lack of) technique or vocal/musical training but in terms of their commitment to an avant-garde/punk aesthetic there are numerous examples in this collection of back catalogues that search the boundaries of the verse-chorus conventions of the pop-song form. There are also many instances of this very form being celebrated even as conventional codes of execution, look, and vocalizing subvert the same. Other differences to what has come to be regarded as a prototypical pop/rock song (in a Beatles song, blues, heavy metal or prog rock for instance) lie in production values, onstage but also in the studio; e.g. inversions of the balance between instruments and vocals, different sorts of guitar tuning (a characteristic of Sonic Youth and Sleater-Kinney), unconventional time-signatures: 'Our songs come out in funny time signatures and structures – and we like it' as Albertine recalls; a characteristic that Chrissie Hynde notes about her own song-writing as well.[99] Experimental and found-object instrumentation also played a role when in the studio, in the Slits' case at least, to provide other sorts of sound effects (e.g. glasses, matches, spoons), rhythmic combinations and resonances in the mix. DIY values in this sense overlap the serendipities of experimentation and joy of making lo-fi music that people want to – and can afford to go and – hear: As Albertine notes the Slits 'were trying to write great pop songs but ended up creating something new by accident.'[100]

Brownstein and Gordon, as well as Smith Start write explicitly about their aims to push the envelope of pop song/guitar rock conventions through musical experimentation; indeed this was the driving force of the Fall in all its incarnations with contributions from all successive band members with or despite the predominance of Mark E Smith's voice and spoken-word musical vision. Albertine, Smith Start, and Gordon go into some detail on the processes, and stresses of recording when dealing with strong personalities, such as Ari Up, Mark E. Smith, or Thurston Moore. Gordon as well as Brownstein and Smith Start concentrate on how songs, as guitar riffs and lyrics, came about as individual and collective processes. Patti Smith discusses the first steps towards her career as singer, rather than poet and essayist, in *Just Kids* but says little about her musical output after that in her memoirs, leaving these reflections on specific work to her interviews.

Let's now take a dive into the 'grain of the voice' in light of the above theoretical excursion, in the authors' own words and by listening to some of the musical output they discuss; as compositions, performances, and recordings.

Patti Smith

> 'And I was slowly becoming enmeshed in the rock world, along with those who inhabited it, through writing and ultimately performing. ... If I was ever going to perform my poems, this was the place to do it. My goal was not simply to do well or hold my own. It was to make a mark at St Mark's. ... I wanted to infuse the written word with the immediacy and frontal attack of rock 'n' roll... Todd [Smith's brother] suggested that I be aggressive, and he gave me a pair of black snakeskin boots to wear. Sam [Shepard] suggested I added music.' (Patti Smith)[101]

Figure 6: Diptych: Kim Gordon and Patti Smith
Artist: Mauricio Escobar (all rights reserved)

Smith is a major figure in this pantheon and its timeline. In her own right but also a point of reference, source of inspiration for other memoirists, if not many a reader. Smith set the bar, as a female poet, musician, and performer as she exemplified a number of key punk visual and sonic tropes. And she does this without actually making punk music as conventionally conceived (back to the Sex Pistols, Buzzcocks, Wire, and American counterparts such as Fugazi, Rancid, or the Ramones with their 3-minute, "fast and furious" tracks). In the passage cited above, one in which the chronological events conjoin with Smith's episodic, dream-sequence style of memoir writing, Smith signals the transition out of her relationship with Robert Mapplethorpe into her time with the playwright Sam Shepard ('Robert was appalled by the thought that Sam was married') and debut as both poet and proto-punk icon in 1971 with her first poetry reading as part of the Poetry Forum events that took place in St Mark's Church ('a desirable forum for even the most accomplished poets').[102] These pages in *Just Kids* provide a clear indication of not only Smith's literary aspirations, but also her ambitiousness in performance terms. They are also a compendium of famous names (less well-known perhaps these days but more than a few are still high-profile) populating overlapping New York beat/punk scenes including those who became part of the Patti Smith Band; Tom Verlaine (1949-2023) for instance, and long-time guitarist Lenny Kaye in particular who provided the guitar backing to her spoken-word debut. Her debut playlist included Kurt Weill and Bertolt Brecht, Jean Genet, as she recalls finishing with her own poem (dedicated to Sam Shepard), 'Ballad of a Bad Boy' that was 'accompanied by Lenny Kaye's strong, rhythmic chords and electric feedback. It was the first time an electric guitar had been played in St Mark's church, provoking cheers and jeers. As this was hallowed ground for poetry...'[103] In one fell swoop,

Smith's first public reading of poetry (hers and that of others) becomes her entrée in the New York underground literary-performance art scene. Phillip Shaw considers this first performance as a blueprint for Smith's signature vocal approach to the 'interface between recital and song... as a visceral experience' and the play list as a precursor to the 1975 album *Horses* which cemented Smith's reputation as punk performer avant-la-lettre.[104]

Viv Albertine writes in her first memoir of when she first saw the photo of Smith on the album cover of *Horses* (released in 1975 and produced by Velvet Underground member, John Cale) and the impact that Smith's vocal delivery and stage presence had on her:

> 'I have never seen a girl who looks like this. She is my soul made visible, all the things I hide deep inside myself that can't come out. She looks natural, confident, sexy and an individual. I don't want to dress like her or copy her style: she gives me the confidence to express myself in my own way. ... I... put the record on. It hurls through stream of consciousness, careers into poetry and dissolves into sex. ... Up until now girls have been so controlled and restrained. Patti Smith is abandoned. Her record translates into sound, parts of myself that I could not access, could not verbalise, could not visualise, until this moment. ... Hearing Patti Smith be sexual, building to an orgasmic crescendo, whilst leading a band, is so exciting. It's emancipating.'[105]

Alice Bag puts it even more explicitly when she recalls seeing Smith play in Los Angeles in 1976, going there 'completely unprepared to have my mind blown, but Patti gave me an unforgettable blow job'. Bag continues as she captures the grain of Smith's embodied *voice*:

> 'She came onstage, a skinny makeup-less wisp of a girl, and before my astonished eyes and ears she transformed herself into a superhuman, androgynous, sensuous, venomous, writhing shaman, spewing words like poison darts that pierced and destroyed my stereotypes. ... Patti completely changed the way I thought about female performers. Most of what I'd seen before her were beautiful women with silky voices. Even those women, who were primarily known for their powerful voices, were repackaged and made over by record companies... Patti was different. Her sensuality came from within. Her power was in her words and in her presence; it didn't come from the sweetness of her voice, because her voice wasn't sweet; her power came from the brutal conviction in it. It didn't come from makeup, high heels, or typically feminine dress; it came from her raw, sexual androgyny.'[106]

These accolades notwithstanding, Smith in her memoirs does not really refer to herself as a punk artist for she considers herself as a poet first and started out that way. She recalls: 'Everything accelerated after Lenny Kaye and I performed at St

Mark's. My ties with the rock community strengthened.' The decisions, deliberate and last-minute, taken in any creative timeline are highlighted in Patti Smith's case, in her recollections at least as she goes on to stipulate that, despite having it suggested to her as a good idea, 'fronting a rock and roll band [was] something that had not occurred to me, or that I had even thought possible. But after writing and performing songs with Sam [Shepard] in *Cowboy Mouth*, I felt the desire to explore songwriting'.[107] Smith recalls this experience with fondness though makes clear that she 'was no actress; I drew no line between life and art. I was the same on- as offstage.'[108]

Smith thereby sees her proto-punk, underground cultural credentials as a musician – songwriter and singer – as happenstance, serendipitous considering the circles in which she was moving and living. This distinguishes her from others in the memoir-set, all of whom *wanted* to be in a band, saw punk as an opening for experimentation, participation, and inclusion in the moment; Chrissie Hynde writes about how desperate she was to find a band to play with for instance. Why Smith's work and persona are so embedded in punkographies has to do with her performance style, the power of her vocals as she controls tempo, rhythm, and build through her (anti-)diction, syllabic and melismatic delivery. But it is also the backing band Smith was to work with for many years, three-four guitarists (Lenny Kaye, Fred [Sonic] Smith, Allen Lanier, and Tom Verlaine) and pianist (Richard Sohl) who Smith soldered into a tight ensemble of counterpoint guitar and keyboard riffs to her elastic declamations. The band were also an integral part to the climactic, "orgasmic" builds that the most well-worn (as in most-played), three-part track on *Horses*, 'Land', exemplifies. Smith's live shows in the period marked out by this album incorporate spoken-word intros, intense shifts in volume from loud to soft that matched Smith's vocal acrobatics that whoop up and down the scale (*portamento*). The ensemble work in which guitar and keyboards sound as vocal parts on the one hand and, on the other, Smith's delivery of words and phrases take on a percussive, rhythmic quality – an aspect under-considered in analyses of Patti Smith as punk icon.[109]

As Shaw notes with perhaps an unfair swipe at musicians such as Joni Mitchell or mega-bands of the time like Supertramp, in these years the 'scene (was) dominated by Laurel Canyon winsomeness and supergroup bombast'[110] which underscores why Smith's onstage persona was so against-the-grain. A video of Smith in 1976 on tour in Europe, where she does a full-out punk cover of the Chubby Checkers 1961 hit, 'Let's Twist Again', makes plain her refusal to move, or sound like her "Laurel Canyon" contemporaries. As Smith's studio recordings morphed from recited poems with musical backing into more familiar rock 'n' roll numbers we can hear how as a songwriter Patti Smith, as well as Chrissie Hynde, works with the conventional lines of rock, faster, 'thrashy' as well as ballad forms in terms of structure – verse, chorus, bridge and variations thereof; minor/major harmonies and melodic lines; 'Because the Night', co-written with Bruce Springsteen, and

'People have the Power' are cases in point. In these registers Smith's lyrics include combinations of rhyming couplets, which differ from the freestyle of her Rimbaud-inflected poetry that conjures up subconscious, trippy visions: For instance, Patti Smith's poem/song 'Wild Leaves', dedicated to Robert Mapplethorpe, is comprised of four eight-line verses – two lots of four lines of an extended couplet; 'Wild leaves are falling – Falling to the ground – Every leaf a moment – A light upon the crown' and so on.[111]

Figure 7: Diptych: Patti Smith
Artist: Mauricio Escobar (all rights reserved)

To round up this consideration of Patti Smith for her vocal influence on punk performativities and developing ideas from Phillip Shaw's – albeit more literary and Lacanian-influenced – 2008 analysis of the *Horses* album, let's consider moments in a live performance from the year that Smith returned to public life. It is 1996, and marks the year that Smith starts touring again, having retreated to the country with her husband to raise two children, travel, read, and write; documented in her *Just Kids* sequel, *M Train*. This come-back tour marks, more or less, her 'middle period' between her arrival in the 1970s and her move towards experimental covers, readings, and gigs at music and literary festivals in recent years. Her work with her daughter, Jesse, on a Nico tribute album encapsulates this latest work (this work is discussed in Chapter Five). Smith has developed an impressive repertoire of covers and these covers where her vocal work is particularly audible; the tracks are well-known, from Bob Dylan and Nirvana to name but two. How Smith achieves and maintains her signature vocals, even as her voice grows older, sounds her "muscular" music, from the body, and to the body, is down to her sung and spoken-word sense of dramatic timing as she builds, crescendos, and then recedes through the song.

The recording of Smith in Hamburg, broadcast on German public radio, exemplifies these qualities, even if she is singing in a more subdued register than in the gigs that Albertine or Bag attended, and other live recordings in her 1970s heyday.[112] It is a gig that revisits her pioneering vocal repertoire and also signals where she was heading in terms of covers (e.g. 'About a Boy' from Nirvana). Along with Lenny Kaye this concert features Tom Verlaine on guitar and it is Verlaine's conversational guitar lines, based on sparse and no-fuss melodic phrases, that stand out in this recording; Smith's return is after the successive deaths of not only her husband, Fred, but also her brother, Todd, including that of Mapplethorpe in 1989. In her spoken-word intermezzo, all about the misadventures of a hat, or hats that Belgian filmmaker, Agnès Varda gifted her delivered in a slow, even hesitant and monotone voice, the weight of grief and, perhaps, rusty stagecraft are audible. Verlaine's guitar also plays a key role in the phrasing and dramaturgy between Smith's vocals and the backing band, which characterizes the *Horses* album, providing the guitar line to Smith's call and response as the song builds. In the Hamburg gig, twenty years later, Verlaine's (Fender Jazzmaster) guitar lines provide another counterpoint to Smith's later renditions of her own hits and covers.

Nina Hagen

> 'I had no idea what to make of the term "punk." But I liked the look of these chaotic figures. Their mangled hairstyles, ripped-up clothes, fishnet stockings and suspenders were a 'fuck you' to the cold commercialism of metropolitan London ... Punks posing as creative scumbags in order to survive. Divine!' (Nina Hagen)[113]

The passage above is from Nina Hagen's memoir, *Bekenntnisse* (*Confessions*), recalling her first sight of punks on the streets of London in the mid-seventies. Published in 2010 so around the same time as Patti Smith's *Just Kids* albeit in German and published for a predominantly European readership, Hagen's memoir is not, as yet, available in English. In this passage she goes on to recall getting to know the Slits, becoming a close friend of Ari Up/Ariane Forster (1962-2010), the Slits lead vocalist, along with other *prominents* in the punk scene at the time; for instance the Sex Pistols (Ari Up's mother, Nora Forster (1942-2023), was married to Johnny Rotten/John Lydon), or music journalist and punk historian, Jon Savage.[114]

Nina Hagen (b. 1955) is a formative representative of the transnational contours of some authors' musico-cultural genealogies; e.g. those of the Slits' founding members such as Ari Up (whose mother was German) and Viv Albertine (whose father was French), or Cosey Fanni Tutti and Throbbing Gristle's time spent with the underground European – German – scenes. Hagen's memoir is, thereby, a particular contribution to a burgeoning public archive that, to date, has been the preserve of Anglo-American artists. Moreover, her observations of the emerging punk scene in London, arriving there after she defected (or, perhaps, was kicked out of East Germany) to West Germany – in light of her own view of what punk stands for on a global level – provide an interesting counterweight to melancholy recollections from British male counterparts. And as a European exponent of the Dadaist theatricality and counter-hegemonic impulse that underpins any (self)designation of punk as anti-establishment, Hagen contributes her own, idiosyncratic iconography to punk-ness as a sustained transborder and multicultural impulse; propelling successive generations of musicians to sound their defiance of cultural authority and commercialism through their respective DIY politics and creative practices. Cosey Fanni Tutti acknowledges Hagen's influence in this regard.[115]

Hagen's singing career began, by her own reckoning, in Poland when she introduced herself to a band based on her past singing experience in choirs, and to the radio. Her repertoire of songs she knew included numbers from Janis Joplin, Joan Baez, Tina Turner, Bob Dylan, and the Doors which seemed to persuade this first line-up that she could sing.[116] In light of this discussion about how punk's grain of the voice matters, and how women whose names are associated with punk have played an under-considered, formative role in the sonography, the Hagen single, 'Unbeschreiblich Weiblich' ('indescribably feminine/female/woman' – take your pick as any one of these are pertinent in translation), from the 1978 *Nina Hagen Band* album she put out with the short-lived band of the same name, provides another register. The sardonic lyrics are about becoming pregnant, about what that means, or what it is supposed to mean in a woman's timeline, and how all these socially imposed, biologically determinist expectations are oppressive.

The track is on first hearing not-strictly-punk when held against the archetypes of British punk bands from the same period. It is a slick, professional three and a half minute track that leans on the synth-keyboard hook, heavy drums and semi-quaver/quaver rhythm of the bass guitar line to join the two verse pairs, with repeated keyboard (ending with its "whoop whoop whoop" upward flourish), together with the refrain. This refrain is where Hagen brings in not only references to Simone de Beauvoir but also Marlene Dietrich as (her) role models for women who rejected the feminine stereotypes of women as child-bearers. The drum rolls, synthesizer sound of a baroque melodic line on keyboards, and studio production values could have been lifted out of a Yes, Tangerine Dream, or Frank Zappa track, none of which fall under the "strictly-punk" rubric. But it is Hagen's vocals, sliding up and down the scale (she can attain low tones as well as the higher soprano register) with the sonic projection and over-diction that are her hallmarks, which are the punk dimension to this track. Nothing about her vocals are poppy; the track ends with the final repeat of the refrain and Hagen's screech of the two syllables 'Weib-**BLICH!**' and then a crash on the hi-hat cymbals. Nina Hagen's rockabilly/punk-inflected version of 'My Way', made famous by Frank Sinatra was recorded around the same time as the infamous Sid Vicious cover. Her 'My Way' went on to be deployed as a triumphant metaphor in live performances on the fall of the Berlin Wall; testament to how a punk-toned voice can overturn the melodic mores of the not-political popular song.[117]

Listen carefully to Nina Hagen's and Patti Smith's vocals side by side and the similarities become more audible. Smith can sing as well. That said, Smith was able, from the outset, to combine conventional – tuneful, pop – vocals with her trademark, melodramatic declamatory delivery that includes lower growl-like timbres, ascending portamento on the *vowels* of selected words, and the higher, soprano register of her younger spoken voice. Critics did not really notice Smith's vocal range until later albums such as *Gung Ho* (2000) which comprise heavy guitar-backed rocky tracks under Smith's more conventionally sung melodies. Both Hagen and Smith express one of the core aesthetic values of punk, a vocal delivery that loudly but also palpably challenges the notion that a song has to be *sung*, meaning in a melodic femininised fashion, to be given credence. Whoops, and jumps up the octave at the upper end of a soprano range are also part of Ari Up's vocals in the Slits' reggae-inflected cover of the Motown hit (with Gladys Knight and then Marvin Gaye) 'I Heard it Through the Grapevine'. In the 1960s and 1970s, pop music positioned female performers as primarily folk singers, singer-songwriter figures, a point that Alice Bag happily rejects after seeing Patti Smith live; these stereotypes had traction despite the volume bellowed out by Grace Slick (lead singer of Jefferson Airplane in the 1960s) or the screams that Janis Joplin made her own. Artists such as Joan Baez and Joni Mitchell, and 'easy-listening' icons such as Karen Carpenter, epitomized the virtuosity of the female global superstar in full voice. Hearing Patti Smith, Nina Hagen, and Ari Up changed the record, then and continues to do so now.

Figure 8: Nina Hagen (reprise)
Artist: Mauricio Escobar (all rights reserved)

Alice Bag

> 'A member of the audience shouts, "Play another song!" I grab the mic stand and shout back into the microphone: "Play my body it's a musical instrument!.."' (Alice Bag)[118]

Alice Bag was raised in a poor Mexican neighbourhood in East LA, forced to learn English at school. The Bag memoir is noteworthy for her stress on the intersection of class, ethnicity, gender, and religion in a life-story interwoven with the early years of the West Coast punk scene as it morphed into hardcore.[119] Her band, the Bags (mostly women and the pun was underscored with their sporting paper bags in their initial aim to remain quasi-anonymous) was also short-lived but Bag provides an understanding of punk as a transborder phenomenon that goes beyond the white, British, male working-class tropes that dominate the historiography. In this respect, her memoir title, *Violence Girl: East L.A. Rage to Hollywood Stage a Chicana Punk Story*, sums up her punk aesthetic and politics. It also puts pay to the specious dichotomies drawn between the incommensurable divide between American women in pop/rock and folk scenes and those women who were drawn to punk. The "Laurel Canyon" trope, the one that Patti Smith is positioned as countervailing voice, coexists uneasily with the barrios of East L.A. and the city's lively punk scene with venues such as Whiskey a Go Go on Sunset Boulevard in Hollywood, the counterpart to New York landmark venues such as CBGB. Bag is keen to put the record straight with regards to what she considers to be a stereotyping of L.A. punk as lightweight.[120]

In this memoir, as the 1970s merge into the 1980s and punk, however defined, becomes more expanded, and more expansive as a genre in marketing terms, Alice Bag reflects on her changes in performance style, her learning curve of discovery about her vocal abilities, the role that 'aggressiveness' played in her delivery onstage but also the violence she encountered at home (a violent parent) and in everyday life and at school as a member of what she realises is an 'ethnic minority' in a deprived suburb. Bag conjures up her first gig and how she embodied her voice, her vocals embodying her coming-of-punk-age thus:

> 'I don't know who introduced us. I don't know what they said, but suddenly I'm onstage and the minute I have the mic in my hand, I become the boxer again, jogging and jumping in place. There's too much energy in my body; I can't control it. The songs start. They're fast. I can't hear myself for a ghost of a voice that seem to come from the back of the room; only it's not a ghost. It's me: That's my voice shrieking, screaming, singing. ... There's so much electricity coursing through my body that I am truly out of control, but I don't care. I couldn't stop myself now if I wanted and the release is like an exorcism – it feels so good.'[121]

There is video footage of Bag fronting the Bags in their most well-known 1978 single, 'Survive'. Her evocation above, of how it felt to be sounding and moving onstage are borne out by her vocals.

Brix Smith Start

The track 'Hotel Bloedel' provides another facet to punk female vocals. Released in 1983 on the Fall's *Perverted by Language* album, this track marks Brix Smith Start's arrival on the band's four-decade timeline. It is one that Smith Start went on to cover years later with her post-Fall band Brix & the Extricated made up of other former Fall members. In the early recording, Smith Start sings, or rather intones, somewhat flatly, the lyrics over a simple a two-chord guitar progression in a minor mode. Mark E. Smith (MES) provides an interpolated spoken-word track. It is catchy, and an uncharacteristically lyrical moment for MES and the band at the time. In the next chapter we will consider how Brix writes about her musical path with the Fall. In 'Hotel Bloedel' it is the voice of Brix that stands out, a departure from the MES growl and scowl vocal. By the time of the later cover in 2016, on the album, *Part 2*, her vocals are more mellow, the melodic line more prominent, the guitar riffs smooth and the drums too. It would be easy to surmise that with this version Brix and her former-Fall colleagues have grown out of their punk-ness. But that is another argument. The point here is that the out-of-tune-ness in the original recording does not detract from the power of her vocal, its timbre, its grain and the tension it sets up against the MES vocal line.

Figure 9: Brix Smith Start (reprise)
Artist: Mauricio Escobar (all rights reserved)

Smith Start is particularly candid about the push and pull between her and Mark E. Smith as a musical partnership. The politics of attribution (song-writing credits) play a major role in the history of the Fall, which affects how to read off the official credits in the extensive online archives about this band by its fans. Smith Start has more than a passing point to make about what it means to be written out of the official credits, and at times out of the final mix in the recording studio. Talking about one of the last albums she was to record with the band, *Frenz Experiment* (1988) – in her mind relatively a commercial success yet 'creative low point' – Smith Start notes that whilst half of the songs on this album are credited to Mark, every 'single one of these songs was a collaboration. It seemed to me that the deterioration of our relationship was reflected in my dwindling song credits.'[122]

Rebel Rebel

'By the time I'm thirty I'll have it all. Isn't that great' (Patti Smith)[123]

'Music, by natural bent, is that which at once receives an adjective. The adjective is inevitable: this music is *this*, this execution is *that*.' (Roland Barthes)[124]

Patti Smith's infectious glee in one of her (many) spoken intermezzi in her early live recordings captures her exuberance in live performance and Barthes' frustration with the 'normal practice of music criticism', cited above, are from the mid-1970s. In the first instance, Smith represents the inception of punk performance as an underground politics in a decade marked by political and social transformations in western societies. Barthes is a prominent representative of literary and philosophical criticism of how western cultural and intellectual establishments engaged with music as an art form; for Barthes this is classical music. Whether Barthes was interested in popular music countercultures or not, his observation about the gap between talking or writing about music as an artefact and experiencing it as a performer or listener holds true across the pop-classical music critical divide.

This chapter has focused on voice, a rubric under which the vocals of the memoirists made a difference to how punk sounds-and-feels, however defined or experienced as performer or fan. The gist of the argument here, and in the next chapters, is that for its exponents, punk encapsulates, in its early years at least, a particular music-making practice which, by definition and display, confronted the hi-fi production and performance values of western classical art music traditions and its 20th century progeny, rock/pop music. Not all punk artists, evidenced in the reflections threaded through the memoir-set, subscribe to the notion of punk as an international *political* movement; stressing, rather, their glee in being part of a cultural phenomenon in which a heterogeneous collection of individuals, bands, and 'scenes' emerged out of capital cities, regional or local underground centres of activity inspired by headliner tours, bootlegs, and the DIY publicity such as 'zines. The memoirs attest to this tension between the particular and the general as they comprise varying renditions of the individual and broader musical-chronologies at work in how authors select tracks, albums or larger projects, for consideration as sonic markers of creative coming-of-age, returns and rediscoveries.

The tension between narratives of punk as a coherent social movement mobilizing around anti-racism, nuclear disarmament and other political causes on the one hand and, on the other, punk as an historical conjuncture, a container term for what were quite disparate acts, needs to be borne in mind when authors recall punk as a spontaneous push back against the 'stale, old, self-indulgent rock establishment' that was to 'coalesce' into a 'global revolution...The wind had carried it [from the East Coast, and the UK] to our western shores', as Alice Bag puts it.[125] Another marker in and out of time is how authorial attributions and acknowledgements unpack the prevailing, rather monolithic notion of a punk politics by their attention to detail, accident, coincidence as fans and then performers with their own followings, record labels, roadies, and managers. Nonetheless, accounts of first bands and first gigs (seen and performed) work across the memoirs as a gendered signifier that troubles the generics of punk as a *masculinised* counterculture; one that serves, too often, as a synonym for the Sex Pistols, the Clash, the Ramones, the Jam, and other male-centred headliner bands.

That which binds the Slits, Sonic Youth, the Fall, and Sleater-Kinney is their conscious experimental impulses within the punk aesthetic of unpolished, off-the-cuff execution. Predating these moments, at the cusp of the late 1960s and early 1970s, Patti Smith was making New York underground poetry rock with electric guitar backing *à la Rimbaud* a hallmark of her early performances and albums, with spoken word still a feature of her live performances. On the other hand, COUM/Throbbing Gristle as Cosey Fanni Tutti relates, were involved in the audio-visuals of the electronic experimental avant-garde from the outset, a timeline that overlaps that of punk. Here electronica, 'industrial' grooves and, similarly to Hagen, Dadaist shock-and-awe embodiments were their sources of inspiration, closer to experimental theatre and performance art in the conventional understandings of Anglo-European underground art-scenes. Meanwhile, the Bags, Selecter, and Pretenders were looking to leverage the zeitgeist challenging (white, western) studio-bound melodic pop-song formalisms. In the case of the Selecter, and the ska/2-tone sound, which they headlined alongside the likes of Madness, and the Specials. Pauline Black and her colleagues were embarking on the (per)sonification of multicultural aspirations for a more just society with their multiracial music making, as Jamaican-inflected beats, sound, look, and stage craft. Chrissie Hynde, as did Kim Gordon, Kim Deal (the Pixies), and Tina Weymouth (Talking Heads) were breaking the mould as lead-bass guitarists in their respective bands.

The next chapter focuses on embodiments that have redefined representations of the performance techniques and punk sonics of woman-with-guitar.

4. GRRRLS WITH GUITARS

Intro

'One afternoon Sam {Shepard} ... took me to a guitar shop in the Village. There were acoustic guitars hanging on the wall, like in a pawnshop, only the cantankerous owner seemed not to want to part with any of them. Sam told me to choose any one I wanted. ... what caught my eye was a battered black Gibson, a 1931 Depression model. ... It was a beautiful gesture that Sam got me the guitar. ... I decided to call the guitar Bo, a short form of Beau. It was to remind me of Sam, who in truth had fallen in love with the guitar himself. Bo, which I still have and treasure, became my true guitar. On it, I have written the greater measure of my songs.' (Patti Smith)[126]

In the passage above Patti Smith conjures up the emotional investment that many exponents have in rock music's star instrument, the electric guitar. It also evokes another, often overlooked dimension to writing about music; the affective relationships that animate music making, a practice too often associated in the literature with individualized hierarchies of creativity and public performance. For the Patti Smith-Sam Shepard relationship, the gift of this musical instrument marks a milestone in their personal lives – with each other, and their other partners – and their collaborative projects combining poetry, improvisational music, and experimental theatre. The romance of 'punk' counterculture (New York style) begins – and ends – in this episode taken from Smith's first memoir, *Just Kids*.

Guitar heroes are the stuff of rock 'n' roll league-tables in the music press, based on plotting (lead) guitarists on a grid of virtuoso technique, synonymous with rapid, if not idiosyncratic finger work (left-handedness for instance), "fretboard mastery" strumming/picking dexterity, and intricate, lengthy improvised solos. For punkographies the guitar also plays a central role in terms of how punk guitar styles, based on the DIY premise and self-identification as non-virtuoso, anti-guitar hero playing, exemplify the alter-ego of mainstream guitar-rock idealizations; *not* how 'Ziggy played guitar' as David Bowie sings in the 1972 *glam rock* classic, 'Ziggy Stardust'. Chrissie Hynde puts the shift in attitude, and aspiration this way:

> 'every band needs songs to play and a shitty original is still better than a good cover – and I had some shitty originals....So when punk bludgeoned its way onto the sagging seventies scene...Everything that went before got thrown on the rubbish heap with no respect or apologies.'[127]

An American, Hynde settled in the UK in the early 1970s, making her career as front woman of the Pretenders, considered a punk band in light of their genesis (1978), overlapping professional networks, musical genealogies and sub-cultural affiliations (Hynde also worked with Vivienne Westwood and Malcolm McLaren, and has been photographed with many of the other authors in this study in their early years). Hynde's memoir is focused on her ambitions as a songwriter, guitarist, and member of a band rather than a solo or lead singer, at least in her early attempts at finding a band to be "in." According to her, the main problem was that 'I did not want to be a solo, singer-songwriter on my own, in any shape or form, or do anything at all other than play the guitar, write songs, and sing as part of a band setup. Being the sole focal point was not the plan.'[128]

The memoirists who took on the guitar, as women and as beginners for the most part, have established their own space of distinction in punk's public archives. Kim Gordon is highly regarded for her bass guitar riffs and their contribution to the Sonic Youth sonic palette. Chrissie Hynde, Brix Smith Start, and Carrie Brownstein developed their own, uncompromising approach to playing guitar for their respective bands using an instrument that has come to embody phallocentric performance values; bass guitar for its low-slung, leg-spreading posture and lead guitar for its complex – ever longer – improvisatorial solos that presaged first-generation punkers' rejection of the prog/glam/stadium idioms of 'cock rock'.[129] Viv Albertine reveals a complex psycho-emotional relationship with her guitar playing while Patti Smith, mainly a vocalist in her live performances, when evoking the guitar as a relational and compositional medium underscores her indebtedness to the distinctive sound of those guitarists she has worked with, Lenny Kaye and Tom Verlaine in particular. Cosey Fanni Tutti for her part, and in her latest writing and recording, takes the guitar back to its sonic frequencies and remixes it through electronic means:

'My Raver guitar was a bit of an odd shape for the way I used it, so me and Chris went and bought another cheap guitar, a Satellite, and worked together on customizing it ... making it easier for me to access the strings with my screwdriver, bottleneck, drumsticks or other objects I wanted to use to make sounds on it. We painted it black. ... I took my guitar to Macari's to try out some FX foot pedals. The other guitarists were all doing renditions of "Stairway to Heaven" and there was me saying to the assistant, "No, I don't need to tune my guitar first – I'll just plug in. I kind of know what sound I'm looking for".'[130]

Figure 10: Cosey Fanni Tutti
Artist: Mauricio Escobar (all rights reserved)

In her 2022 track 'Guitar', the guitar in this Cosey-after-Throbbing Gristle incarnation is rendered as manipulated electro(acoustic) remix rather than (male) embodiment of pop/rock virtuosity. All the more reason to consider how our memoirists also discuss their own music-making, guitar encounters, and (self)perceptions of playing on stage brandishing a guitar in ways associated with Dee Dee Ramone (the Ramones), Sid Vicious (the Sex Pistols), Keith Levene (the Clash and then Public Image Ltd), or Mick Jones (the Clash) let alone all those male rock 'n' roll guitar heroes who continue to 'walk this way'. This chapter unpacks some of the authors' discussions and recollections of playing as beginners and then more experienced and confident musicians in light of an ongoing sub-text; that punk discourses and playlists are framed by a certain *counter-hypermasculinity* of performance. The focus is on how authors consider selected tracks from their back catalogues. As is the case with voice (see Chapter 3), playing electric (bass) guitar against the main-malestream is about holding the floor, and body in a sonic space full of others all too willing to show you how much more 'skilful' they are as instrumentalists.

Guitars Guitars Guitars

Here is one way to play guitar: 'When I hear an element within a sound that "speaks" to me I filter out everything else until I find that "golden nugget." When I'm playing guitar I use the band-pass filter in my wah-wah pedal to eliminate everything until I get the partial frequency and tone I want for my guitar sound.'[131] Cosey is conveying how she plays (with a) guitar, as an instrument to produce sonic frequencies for digital sampling and remixing, a far cry it would seem from mainstream popular music's electric guitar pyrotechnic displays. Her not-strictly-punk approach to the guitar underscores how the instrument has remained a primary vehicle for experimentation in the history of pop music instrumentation. The guitar is also central to the sound-world of punk rock, albeit with a repertoire of countermanding techniques that challenges the stereotype of punk being non-committal, non-rehearsed music making. David Pearson in his study of US punk rock scenes, argues against the notion that punk as a musical style implies easy-to-play instrumental techniques. He notes:

> 'While...amateurism and the low bar for participation are central to punk, ... performing punk nevertheless required the development of specific musical techniques – such as fast strumming and rapidly shifting from one power chord to the next for the guitarist; fast heavily accented playing and hitting the hi-hat in just the right place for the drummer; and just the right sneer for the vocalist ... The "sloppiness" some hear in punk music is not just or even mainly a matter of amateurishness, but the cultivation of musical techniques... that deliberately create a seemingly sloppy sound...in many cases a result of hours of practice to achieve that effect.'[132]

Such conventions gravitate around guitar riffs based on power chords – rather than fast, tricky melodic riffs of guitar-heroes of yore, a 'fast rock beat, with strong snare-drum hits on beats two and four – the "backbeat" of rock, with tempi that were initially at 150-180 bpm and up to 200bpm and 'abrasive', slurred and out-of-tune vocals.' It is Pearson's contention that punk denotes a *musical* style with a repertoire that warrants concerted musicological analysis. He goes on to note how musicians conversant with mainstream pop music idioms do not find punk's repertoire of performance techniques self-evident:

> 'Betraying the cultivation of techniques necessary for (im)proper punk musicianship is the fact that when musicians trained, including formally, in other styles of music attempt to play punk, they must unlearn their previous technique and adopt a new approach to playing their instrument.'[133]

That playing punk *well* also requires *practice* does not detract from how its burgeoning repertoire of performance techniques sets punk apart in the 20th century rock music canon of virtuoso guitar-playing. Thrashy power-chords, raspy snarly vocals, and the oft-cited 'simple three-chord' harmonic progressions that 'anyone can play' demarcate the diversity of styles that fall under the punk rubric as much as they delineate generations of musicians who came before, and after UK '77-style punk' grabbed media headlines.[134]

Our memoirists evoke these features in their recollections of learning to play punk-style, loosely defined; note that the Slits were steeped in dub-reggae musical idioms which do not "do" power chords as such and this was the context in which Viv Albertine honed her early guitar sound. Brix Smith Start's love of 'poppy' riffs when she joined the Fall in 1983 irritated Fall fans devoted to the discordant, discontinuous guitarisms over the driving basslines (from Fall bassists, Marc Riley and Steve Hanley) that underscored Mark E. Smith's spoken word throughout the band's multiple personnel changes. While a celebration of DIY creative practices does not mean that any ensuing techniques are achievable without putting in some modicum of practice, the prevalence of masculinist tropes pivoting on DIY as immediate, 'natural' musical prowess is underscored by the numerical predominance of males playing hard, very fast, and with rhythmic intensity ("power"); key to mainstream punk's back catalogue and, for the most part, research literature. All-male groups such as the Ramones are frequently extolled for their exemplification of these performance codes and techniques that were the result of hours of 'drilling their songs at band practices.'[135]

Authors like Kim Gordon, Chrissie Hynde, Carrie Brownstein, and Viv Albertine encapsulate the sonics of *gender trouble* – to borrow from Judith Butler's proposition that gender, like many other aspects of everyday life, is not a given but, rather, is a 'performative' practice. For the memoirists the performativity conundrum lies between their experience as audience and their aspirations as (wannabe) punk exponent: between their not seeing any women playing electric guitar, being enthralled by men with guitars while not daring to envision themselves on stage playing (electric) guitar themselves.[136] Albertine articulates the emotional dialectic for her part this way:

> 'Every cell in my body was steeped in music, but it never occurred to me I could be in a band, not in a million years – why would it? Who'd done it before me? There was no one I could identify with. No girls played electric guitar. Especially not ordinary girls like me.'[137]

Kim Gordon articulates such tensions between execution and perception of a performance, when considering the life – and death (from anorexia nervosa) – of Karen Carpenter, a musician with a deep contralto voice who also excelled in playing the drums in her brother-sister 'polished-pop' duo (see Chapter Two). In a chapter reflecting on her motivation for writing 'Tunic (Song for Karen)', Gordon considers some of the body politics for female musicians:

> 'The Carpenters were such a sun-drenched American dream, such a feel-good family success story like the Beach Boys, but with the same rolling darkness going on underneath. ... The only autonomy Karen felt she had in her life she exerted over her own body. She was an extreme version of what a lot of women suffer from – a lack of control over things other than their bodies, which turns the female body into a tool for power – good, bad, or ugly.'[138]

Punkographies that consider the sexual politics of selected punk scenes, and to which Carrie Brownstein's memoir provides a cogent response from centre-stage, still beg the question of whether women – as embodied females – can play according to the exigencies of techniques embedded in, what Pearson notes was, the '*increasing* masculinity of the punk and hardcore scenes': or whether women aspiring to punk-guitar prominence would want to do so.[139] Some practitioners recall being concerned about the higher pitch of their voices in terms of punk's vocal repertoire, underscored in Alice Bag's memoir (see Chapter Three).[140] A masculinist performative norm persists as the default setting for those bands deemed influential to the legacy of punk as a global politico-cultural phenomenon, its Anglo-American myth of origins notwithstanding.

The authors revisit selected tracks or significant others (colleagues, friends, and lovers), revealing how a spectrum of *contested* masculinities has always been an issue, for both "she-punks" and "he-punks." between the gender-bending of glam rock icons like Marc Bolan or (early) David Bowie, say, on the one hand and, on the other, the paroxysms of Led Zeppelin guitar solos or hi-speed chords of the Ramones. As the riot grrrl phenomenon within a feminist punk/punk feminist consciousness took shape in 1990s post-punk scenes on the US riot grrrl bands, like Bikini Kill and Sleater-Kinney, along with Alice Bag and her first band, the Bags, or her second band, Suicide Squad, were contending with the music industry and music press perpetuating musicmaking as quintessentially a male domain. Alice Bag, Kim Gordon, Viv Albertine, Cosey Fanni Tutti, and Pauline Black are particularly astute about the psychopathologies of performance from the men around them, let alone the rank sexism and condescension of the music press, and fans. These attitudes all too casually intersected with incipient racism, cross-cutting experiences that Bag and Black make plain in their respective memoirs.[141]

Bodies Bodies Bodies: Woman with Guitar

'Since our music can be weird and dissonant, having me centre-stage also makes it that much easier to sell the band. *Look, it's a girl, she's wearing a dress, and she's with those guys, so things must be okay.* But that's not how we had ever operated as an indie band, I was always conscious not to be too much out front.' (Kim Gordon)[142]

'I wanted to play rhythm, not so much because I thought it was easier than lead, but because rhythm turned me on. I'd never once been tempted to play a single note. Chords for me, three; less is more.' (Chrissie Hynde)[143]

What punk as a critical musico-cultural impulse with political ambitions – to engage in movements for systemic change (anti-capitalist), social justice (anti-racism, gay rights), and political platforms (environmentalist, anarchist, or socialist) – did establish is that *anyone* can get *started*, get a band together and play live without being pitch-perfect, or particularly adept in terms of finger-work or power-chord strumming. But sustaining punk music making within a performance culture still dominated by male-embodiments of excess and prowess remains a leitmotiv through these women's accounts of their early careers. With the two observations from Kim Gordon and Chrissie Hynde in mind, a brief visit to the proximate past of women playing guitar and becoming iconic is appropriate for that reason. By this I am referring to the path that Suzi Quatro broke open with her leather-clad, heavy-cum-glam rock bass guitar playing in the 1970s. Vocalist and song-writer in her own right, Quatro's public persona and the way she brandished a *bass* guitar – a larger instrument associated with taller men in the annals of rock bass guitar-heroes – was formative. With the first-wave of punk and its so-called *new wave* successors women playing bass – such as Tina Weymouth (b. 1950) from Talking Heads, Kim Deal (b. 1961) from the Pixies and then, later, the Breeders, or Poison Ivy (b. Kristy Marlana Wallace, 1953) from the Cramps – form a cohort in which Kim Gordon is a key figure.

Such accounts evoke yet do not completely endorse aspects of the feminist politics that was gathering momentum in the 1970s. Not all the authors identify as *feminists* as such. In some cases, they distance themselves from feminist politics, and feminist academe, Cosey Fanni Tutti in particular. How to think further about a woman brandishing a guitar in a punk-cum-masculine fashion or simply appearing on stage with this instrument, playing it in ways that challenged the 'folksy' acoustic styles of prominent female musicians of the time, has been enhanced by shifts in feminist scholarship along an intertwined timeline to that of the memoirs. To continue along the conceptual line of thinking thus far, these debates pivot on Butler's concept of performativity through *embodiment*, manifesting at the intersection of sexuality, gender, class, and race: one example of how some of these dynamics are played out in contemporary pop culture is on the Reality TV franchise, *RuPaul's Drag Race*.[144]

The shift, in activist emphasis and empirical focus for feminist scholars from Second Wave to so-called Third Wave feminism is not uncontroversial within the ongoing history of women's rights activism and policy advocacy. I will return to these discussions about the form and content of feminist politics and research in due course. The point of note when considering how the authors write about their selected tracks, and how a listener might encounter them, is that considering the intricacies of gendered embodiment through public music making performance allows space for considering, as Peraino argues, 'how music– rock no less, and perhaps more – demarcates a space and time wherein gender and sexuality lose clear definition. ... this is part of music's appeal and cultural work. The fact that men dominate the world of rock and pop does not mean that music itself uncomplicatedly represents masculinity, as many 1970s feminists held.'[145] The memoirists here articulate these sex-gender nomenclatures in complex, at times contradictory but, always, in defiant ways.

Viv Albertine

> 'Listening to T. Rex was one of the first times I actually noticed guitar playing (apart from Peter Green and George Harrison). Bolan's riffs were so catchy and cartoony – combined with a very distinctive guitar sound – that I would find myself singing the parts. Girls didn't usually listen out for guitar solos and riffs, that was a male thing – *wow that was so fast, wow that was a really obscure scale, wow the way he bends the notes*. I used to listen to the lyrics and the melody of songs, not dissect the instruments. I couldn't bear Hendrix's playing at the time, it was so in your face and he was so overtly sexual, it was intimidating.' (Viv Albertine)[146]

All these contradictions are evident in Albertine's recollection of the guitar work from Marc Bolan's T. Rex (a pin-up for young men and women at the time); the gender-bending on stage that defines glam rock is part of the double-edged context of sex-gender roles in the mid-twentieth century of pop music's heartlands. But it also kept many women in their bedrooms (as fans and music consumers) and on the edges of public discourse about music trends in which men did the gender-bending and male pundits set the tone for audience appreciation.

Albertine devotes a chapter to her encounter with guitar in the 1970s, entitled 'First Guitar'. On inheriting some money, Albertine recalls that instead of spending it on a motorbike she decided that she would buy a guitar, a decision triggered by her seeing the Sex Pistols. She tells her (then) boyfriend Mick (Jones of the Clash) that she was 'going to buy a guitar. An electric guitar'. Like Patti Smith before her, Albertine recollects the experience of shopping for this first guitar, the intensity of her decision as she encounters the 'sneery' and 'impatient' shop assistant, feeling increasingly like 'a fool' as she and Mick confer over which guitar would suit her best. Albertine is bucking convention in sentiment and in deed. She is effectively transgressing a socially defined masculinized space – the electric guitar shop – by entering it, not as girlfriend or onlooker, but as a customer:

> 'I'm a twenty-two-year-old girl who's never had a music lesson and never touched a guitar. Everyone I've heard of who plays electric guitar is male and has paid their dues by starting out on acoustic, which I can't be bothered to do.'[147]

Albertine's account underscores the gender-power relations imbued in discourses and personae around electric guitar-*man*-ship, part of the 'impenetrable iron door that is convention' which she was determined to 'dart through'. Albertine is also staking her claim, in retrospect, for how punk 'pushed open' these figurative and visceral barriers to women taking ownership of music making and musical instruments in ways not always defined by extraordinary technical prowess. Music scholarship and journalism have noted those women whose virtuosity marked them apart, Clara Schumann for instance in the romantic period of classical art music, or Nina Simone, as a classically trained, jazz-blues-gospel concert pianist, but as exceptions within these male pantheons, not examples of "ordinary" musicianship. Albertine continues in this vein:

> 'It has to be the guitar. The look, the size, the shape it's all recognizable to me...I like the way the guitar weaves and chops through the other instruments. I know that I'm not grounded and steady enough to play bass, not outgoing and confident enough to be a singer. I need an instrument to direct my emotions through. A little distance. The size of the strings and neck suit my fingers and the frequency of the notes is familiar, near to the pitch of my own voice. The guitar resonates with how I talk...It just feels right. No question. It couldn't be any other instrument.'[148]

All this determination is recalled in this passage, before Albertine has even held a guitar let alone learned to play one. Eventually, following Mick Jones's advice Albertine buys a 'single-cutaway sunburst 1969 Les Paul Junior...the right size, shape and weight...It's simple and classy. It's a serious guitar.'[149]

In between the top of this passage and its resolution Albertine expresses in some detail what sort of sound she was looking for, and who from other groups inspired her; John Cale's electric violin and viola sounds from the Velvet Underground are what she wants to evoke in her playing, on guitar. She also notes the sorts of structures and sequences she is not trying to emulate, 12-bar blues for instance. Next to Carrie Brownstein, Albertine is the only memoirist who goes into this depth about the phenomenology of playing an instrument according to performance codes that push back against mainstream techniques and sounds. Unlike the other memoirists, however, Albertine finds it all hard going: 'I just wish I loved playing guitar. I thought you were supposed to love playing music, that it's a release and a comfort, that's what other musicians say. For me, it's agony.'[150] Her account contrasts to those of Chrissie Hynde and Brix Smith Start for not only is it a slow and arduous process to master some sort of technique but more so as Albertine is on a mission:

> 'Expressing myself through the guitar is a very difficult concept to grasp. I don't want to copy any male guitarists... Slowly I start shaping a guitar style, twisting strands together, layering then undoing and starting again, until I start to sound like me.'[151]

It also underscores that under-acknowledged rehearsal dimension to punk music making, running counter to the public discourses and media stereotypes of these early bands, and their successors in subsequent waves and derivatives. It also echoes the "agony" of learning to play any instrument when not naturally endowed – after all not everyone is a multi-talent like Stevie Wonder, Prince, or Joni Mitchell. Albertine is making a statement about role models, a certain sort of *hegemonic masculinity* (I am referring here to R. W. Connell's contribution to debunking essentialist notions of masculinity) that music industry moguls, and some pundits, favour in terms of contracts and reviews.[152] For this is a practitioner with a philosophy of punk musicianship. By the end of the 1970s and now established as a major act through her time with the Slits, Albertine notes how she is maturing in her playing and knowledge of the other dimensions to making music:

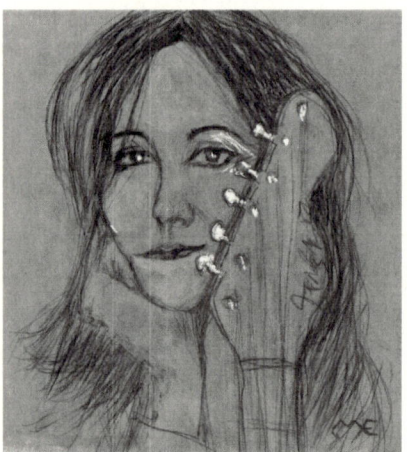

Figure 11: Viv Albertine (and guitar)
Artist: Mauricio Escobar (all rights reserved)

'My guitar style is developing into its own sound even more now I know what I am listening for when I hear a record. I'm moving away from the buzzsaw, industrial whine I was developing with Keith {Levene}. I still don't have any female guitarists to listen to and be inspired by, and I hate the note-bending, flashy solos, posturing and lip pursing of a lot of male rock guitarists, but I've found some I like. ... I didn't like Led Zeppelin or Hendrix, any heavy rock, it felt masculine and unappealing.'[153]

Albertine's theory of electric guitar performance values expresses a particular sort of feminist politics of punk musicianship. How she sounds, and why she sounds that way within the mark that punk styles made on popular music at the time, and since, are fundamental to Albertine's coming of age as an 'ordinary girl' who also 'played guitar'. She does despite the 'obsessive listening and repetitive exposure to songs about idealized love' characterizing for her 'how girls listened to songs... about romantic love.'[154]

The Slits – 'So Tough' (Cut, 1979)

Albertine's reflections on her efforts learning to play electric guitar are part of her account of how the Slits' first album in 1979, *Cut*, took shape in the studio, under the tutelage of dub/reggae producer Derek Bovell and leadership of the teenage Ari Up. Considered – by Albertine herself and critics – their best work *Cut* included the band's first recording, their take on 'I heard it through the Grapevine' as a bonus track; ground-breaking musically for the use of reggae and African beats, improvised instrumentation, the vocal style of Ari Up's not-quite-singing in tune, and Viv Albertine's guitar and backing vocals. This album also had its visual impact, the (in)famous record cover, also recalled in Hynde's memoir, of the three band-members topless, covered in mud and in a sort of "jungle" attire. Chapter 54 entitled 'Cut' takes the reader through each track, one by one. The track. 'So Tough', is a good example of their vocal style, discussed in Chapter Three. The lyrics draw from a conversation Albertine had with John Lydon (Johnny Rotten) from the Sex Pistols about Sid Vicious and his deteriorating wellbeing. Albertine notes that she tried to make a guitar riff she already had fit the words. The eventual repeating of this original motif in this riff is attributed to Sid himself. It was his suggestion to 'repeat the first part of the riff, do it twice... a great idea and I liked that he contributed to the song about himself'. Albertine notes later, also with respect to the hit track 'Typical Girls', that she had to practise the songs, and her own guitar riffs in order to remember them the next day as she cannot write music.[155]

'So Tough' opens with voices (Ari Up and Viv Albertine) muttering, and then half-humming the refrain in a sort of buzzing effect, over the 4/4 beat of the drums; 'He had fun experience – Nothing he does ever makes sense – He is only curious – Don't take it serious'. At this point the riff in question enters (20" into the track) for the first verse of the three verses. This first verse has four lines interspersed with two, backing vocal phrases, 'so tough' (twice) and 'so hard' (twice). The second verse has eight lines, more snippets of the Lydon-Albertine conversation, punctuated with 'so strong' (twice), 'too long' (twice), 'too much' (twice), 'too fast', 'slow down' sung in a descending scale: the conversation juxtaposed with asides (so tough, so hard, so strong, too long, too fast, slow down). The guitar riffs links in to and builds from the chorus (repeated four times). With each reiteration the musical, rhythmic, and vocal shapes differ as the last phrase ('Don't take it serious') repeats as a build-up to then release into the next verse. The song ends with a coda combining lines from the chorus and verses, ending with the final phrase 'don't take it serious' three times; Albertine's reggae-based strum builds to the abrupt ending at the end of the third, and loudest declamatory 'DON'T TAKE IT SER-I-OUS' in dissonant harmonies, to finish with the recapitulation of the muttering voices from the intro.

The track is two minutes and forty-one seconds of a tightly crafted "pop song" with minimalist instrumental backing, two guitar-lines on two tracks, with drums played by guest drummer, Budgie (Peter Clarke, later of Siouxsie and the Banshees). His contribution to the album is something that Albertine considers an important ingredient to her satisfaction with the record, because of the way Budgie's 'presence transforms the dynamic between us', noting that it was 'great to suddenly have this male energy in the room.' Make of this statement what you will from a strictly feminist point of view, but Albertine's point underscores the disconnect between the person and punk persona of Sid Vicious which drives the track, and the input of Budgie as a drummer. Albertine acknowledges how Budgie

> 'has a light touch, is rock-steady and, most important of all, has no problem whatsoever with Ari giving him extremely detailed instructions about the rhythms, the hi-hat patterns and no cymbal bashing. He's respectful and confident. Ari's getting stronger and stronger musically and needs a drummer who can play her vision as well as add his own ideas and technique. ...to be able to take that from a sixteen-year old girl who doesn't play drums, that takes a very special person.'[156]

Brix Smith Start

Turning now to how Brix Smith Start looks back at her time with the Fall, divided into two periods, her relationship with founder of the Fall, Mark E. Smith as well as her time with the Fall's fanbase, who were less than enthusiastic about her 'commercial' influence.

'US 80's 90's' (Bend Sinister, 1986)

This album is one in which Smart Smith talks about her sense of a deterioration in Mark E. Smith's vision of writing, and then recording songs as live improvisation. This aspect to how he controlled Fall tracks as the outcomes of conscious 'first takes', with mistakes not edited out of the final mix, is an integral aspect to what Smith Start considers the essence of the Fall's sound. It is also, to her mind, integral to the continuity of Smith's hold on the band despite innumerable changes in line-ups: 'Leaving in the mistakes, insisting on first takes, simplifying arrangements to the most elemental, tribal cacophony...aren't recipes for brilliance, but herein the magic lies'. Her verdict on this album is that despite Mark E. Smith's 'edicts [not] coming from an objective musicality, but from a strange, angry place' the final result 'isn't bad, by any means, but it could have been incredible.'[157.] These sections also relate the various episodes of band-members being thrown out of the band whilst touring and, then, the band turning around and basically throwing Mark E. Smith himself out of the band. The point here is that Smith's on-stage and in the studio habits of intervening with other band members while they played cannot be separated from the effects this sort of "Dadaist" (Smith Start calls it self-destructive) approach to making and mixing music *in situ* has on the sound of the Fall, as one articulation of DIY as unpredictability. According to Smith Start, their move into writing opera, and with that dance soundtracks (released in 1988 as *I am Kurious Oranj*) imposed an external discipline on this behaviour, and the album of that music that ensued.

Smith Start talks about how the lyrics of 'U.S. 80's-90's' draw on an experience of being interrogated about prescription pills at US Customs in Boston, generating their 'own version of a hip-hop track' in which 'Mark proclaims 'I am the original white (big shot) rapper'. The track is based on a repetitive, 'blistering and hypnotic' combination of rhythm that opens with a standard 4/4 drum intro; two main riffs from both lead and bass guitar back the spoken-singing style that also characterizes Mark E. Smith's vocals as he recounts, and meta-comments on this episode.[158] He never sings in the conventional sense of the word; rather, he intones over the music backing in all the Fall's line-ups, ones that include two drummers, bass guitar, keyboards, lead and rhythm guitar and (Smith Start often singing) backing vocals in various combinations and registers.

Smith Start considers the riff on this track as a heavier example of her riff-writing[159]; based on her adapting her playing to what she considered would 'go really well with what [the Fall] were doing and develop this kind of lead guitar technique – very hooky, simple, powerful, leads.'[160] The hook in the song is the title, sung as refrain with a two-tone bass rhythm. The riff that Smith Start speaks of enters at 10" into the track, a rocky, melodic lead-guitar line that provides the hook. Additional sound effects are provided by Smith's 'idiotic megaphone' (discernible towards the end of the track at 3.33).[161] Four minutes and forty seconds of recitation held together by a bass-guitar and lead-guitar riff and a solid 4/4 drumbeat.

Kim Gordon

> 'After thirty years of playing in a band, it sounds sort of stupid to say, "I'm not a musician." But for most of my life I've never seen myself as one and I never formally trained as one. I sometimes think of myself as a lowercase rock star. Yes, I'm sensitive to sound, I think I have a good ear, and I love the visceral movement and the thrill of being onstage. And even as a visual, conceptual artist, there's always a performance aspect to whatever I do. For me, performing has a lot to do with being fearless.' (Kim Gordon)[162]

In contrast to the other authors, Kim Gordon made her way as a bassist in the group she co-founded with Thurston Moore, Sonic Youth. This instrument brings with it an additional edginess when wielded by a female body; a transgressive sexuality that ran counter to media representations of women musicians was already palpable in the persona of Suzi Quatro. Gordon, like Chrissie Hynde, is unapologetic about the sexual charge that comes with playing electric (bass) guitar on stage, and as the only woman. She is less inclined to articulate a clear (queer) feminist line of thought than does Carrie Brownstein (Sleater-Kinney was two guitars and drums, no bassist). The recollection below from Gordon countermands mainstream, liberal feminist theories of sex-gender power relations as necessarily oppressive for female subjectivities: It is complex stuff that Gordon conjures up in this passage, which she published as an article entitled 'Boys are Smelly' for the *Village Voice* in the 1980s:

> 'Before picking up a bass I was just another girl with a fantasy. What would it be like to be right under the pinnacle of energy, beneath two guys crossing their guitars, two thunderfoxes in the throes of self-love and male bonding? How sick, but what desire could be more ordinary? ... In the middle of the stage, where I stand as a bass player of Sonic Youth, the music comes at me from all directions. The most heightened state of being female is watching people watch you. Manipulating that stage, without breaking the spell of performing, is what makes someone like Madonna all the more brilliant. ... For many purposes, being obsessed with boys playing guitars, being as ordinary as possible, being a girl bass player is ideal, because the swirl of Sonic Youth music makes me forget about being a girl. I like being in a weak position and making it strong.'[163]

In this admission, even if for a piece written tongue-in-cheek one could surmise, Gordon is making plain that women – "girls" – could fantasize – and make these fantasies reality – about playing guitar, any which way and that need not be 'extraordinary'.

'Little Trouble Girl' (Washing Machine, 1995)

Chapter 35 of Gordon's *Girl in a Band* focuses on Sonic Youth's 1995 album, *Washing Machine*, which coincides with the birth of Gordon and Moore's daughter, Coco. Some songs on this album reflect Gordon's concerns with parenthood, such as 'Little Trouble Girl'. Here too we hear another example of vocals based on 'half singing, half speaking style' to deliver lyrics such as 'cross my heart and hope to die, I cannot tell a lie' (at 3.33) as her 'homage' to the Shangri-Las and their 'over-dramatic songs with morbid scenarios and unhealthy relationships.'[164]

It is a track that includes backing vocals from Kim Deal singing a melodic line – 'sha la la'. Gordon considered Deal as 'perfect' for this song about the 'pressure to please and be perfect that every woman falls into and then projects onto her daughter.'[165] The darker sentiments in the lyric are contrasted by Deal's melodic line, and the quality to her voice that Gordon describes as having 'an incredibly cakelike quality – like the sound when you say *cake*, a lightness, its body thinned out. That's so classic pop.'[166] An arpeggio line on the lead guitar plays in unison with the two vocalists, singing almost but not quite in tune with each other for the first verse that ends with' – that I'm really bad, little trouble girl' over a slow 2/4 drumbeat. A slight echo-chamber effect contributes to the sense of foreboding and strangeness that Gordon evokes in her notes for this track. It is a gentle-sounding song without the feedback, grunge-sounding guitars of other Sonic Youth tracks. But this is the point, the sonic dissonances and sense of unease are subtle through slightly off-key harmonies and guitar lines that wobble in pitch at the end of the phrase (4.07-4.09). The album title, the title track of which is over 9 minutes long, could have been the new name for the band. Gordon here is commenting on the need for a change as the band had 'been around awhile, plus *Washing Machine* seemed like a good "indie rock" name.'[167] These branding concerns aside she notes that recording this album included having her daughter Coco, a toddler at the time, in the studio and is one of her 'favourite sounding records' of 'fun songs to record.'[168]

Figure 12: Diptych: Carrie Brownstein and Kim Gordon
Artist: Mauricio Escobar (all rights reserved)

In a later venture after Sonic Youth (and the end of her marriage to Thurston Moore), a collaborative experimental project with Bill Nace entitled Body/Head premised on improvisation, Gordon returns to the theme of female-bodies-guitars from within the performance sonic-space: 'The best kind of music comes when you're being intuitive, unconscious of your body, in some ways losing your mind'. And with this insight, towards the end of her memoir as her own music and writing pathways develop new directions, Gordon expresses a matured performance ethics: not necessarily improvisation for this later venture but, rather, '... eccentric noise/rock music as opposed to, say, performance art, which is a term I loathe.'[169] With this flourish Gordon claims the sonic and visceral space at the intersection of womanhood (however defined) and punkishness (as a craft) for all-comers.

Carrie Brownstein

> 'There was a thunderous greeting from the crowd; it was a "HELLO" so enormous I could climb inside. And I did. ... I was in my body, joyous and unafraid. I was home.' (Carrie Brownstein)[170]

Brownstein ends her memoir with Sleater-Kinney reuniting in 2012, the 'first time Janet, Corin, and I played music together after six years apart...in Corin's basement'. After a decade they record the 2015 album, *No Cities to Love*, taking it on tour in smaller venues at first, 'begin on the fringes if we could', and discovering that their global fanbase would be welcoming their comeback. The final passage in the book, cited above, ends Brownstein's homage in this chapter to the intertwining of the earlier creative and personal relationships with her two bandmates and their respective lifepaths since Sleater-Kinney's first successes and at times uneasy affiliation with riot grrrls rhetoric.[171]

The first chapter of Part 2 in Brownstein's *Hunger Makes Me a Modern Girl*, entitled 'Sleater-Kinney', introduces the reader to how their sound worked; first as a three piece without a bass guitar and, second, as a three piece with two vocalists and guitarists working closely together, in unison and alternating. Brownstein notes that neither she nor Corin Tucker 'were interested in playing too many bar or power chords. So my chords were half-formed; I was always trying to leave room for Corin. ... a story that on its own sounds unfinished, a sonic to-be-continued, designed to be completed by someone else.'[172] As with the other bands examined above, their guitar tunings were not standardized;

> 'had always tuned her guitar to her own voice ... [for example] in C-sharp...one and a half steps below standard tuning, which creates a sourness, a darkness that you have to overcome if you're going to create something at all harmonious and palatable, So, even when we're getting toward a little bit of catchiness or pop sheen,

there's always an underlying bitterness to it. The tuning also forced Corin to sing differently – it pushed her into her higher registers, into a wailing, the outer edges.'[173]

In this account, the circumstances of tuning a guitar to fit the natural range of a voice, without deference to conventions, is behind the sonic qualities of this band. Once they had found their first drummer (Janet Weiss), Brownstein maintains that they did not need to add a bass player for the obligatory 'depth and low end' despite wanting to 'sound like a full rock band'. The sonic effect of 'ways of playing that were very compatible with each other' and the intensity of Weiss's drumming fuses the counterpoint of the two vocalists and their intertwined guitar lines. Brownstein reckons that 'the uniqueness of our sound is that we rarely land on a basic chord – the music stays somewhere in between, it's always not quite right, which of course can sound more right than anything, or at least like nothing else.'[174]

'Faraway' (One Beat, 2002)

How does this work out for the album *One Beat*, in the three minutes and forty-five seconds of 'Faraway'? The track evokes first reactions to hearing about the 9/11 attacks, and their geopolitical aftermath. Brownstein is quite clear on the political position they were taking towards the George W. Bush administration in this instance for a band with members, unlike other authors in the memoir-set, openly identified with the 1990s feminist politics encapsulated by riot grrrl bands.[175]

The first verse goes like this; 'Seven thirty a.m.- Nurse the baby on the couch -Then the phone rings -Turn on the TV – Watch the world explode in flames – And don't leave the house'. No musical intro in this track, the first line begins on the 4th beat of the first bar, both guitars in unison with drums in full throttle and Tucker's 'wailing' vocals around two-three notes. The second verse follows the first after a brief link with guitar (1.02), which follows the same intervals of this melodic line. The song takes off in the middle section (1.14), upping the tempo with the two vocal lines separating into lead and backing to come together again on the main refrain 'Why can't I get along – Why can't I get along – Why can't I get along with you?' (Sung twice). The last minute, a third of the song, consists of repeated variations of the main riff, to finish off with a *da capo* to the second part of the main verses (3.11); 'Standing here on a one way road – And I fall down, and I fall down – No other direction for this to go- And we fall down, and we fall down' and four bars of guitars in unison to the end. This song is one good example of exactly the points Brownstein is making above as they looked to sound like a full line-up, eschewing a 'lo-fi trebly noise...each used to compensating yet unafraid of space or discord.'[176] It works on its own terms and within the terms of a three to four-minute verse-chorus structured pop song albeit with their own style of sonic arc and harmonies: drive, build and release.

Punk Musica Practica

'1. Don't play guitar like anyone else.... 31. Guitars can howl, yowl, shriek, sputter, scream, dream, steam, shatter sonic boom bash, crash, sing, sting and cry but they will not twitter.' (Thurston Moore)[177]

'The music I was exposed to when I was growing up was revolutionary and because I grew up with music that was trying to change the world, that's what I still expect from it.' (Viv Albertine)[178]

The first citation above is taken from a string of tweets, on the social media platform formerly known as Twitter, about guitar-playing from Thurston Moore, co-founder of Sonic Youth with (ex-partner) Kim Gordon. Albertine, for her part, moves from recalling her beginner-anxiety to a more articulated position on how music and politics can be mutually reinforcing fields of endeavour. The latter claim is more often asserted than it is explained, if 'musicking politics' implies something more than explicitly politically engaged lyrics.[179] In order to consider how music making can implicate a political expressivity of agency – personal, community, or institutional – we need to revisit theories of music as high culture.

In Chapter Three I considered how Roland Barthes and his thinking on the tension between encountering music through the body and analysis as a cerebral project offers ways into how women in punk's early years had to find their voice. Here I will pay another visit to Barthes on music in terms of how the memoirists articulate their relationships – physical and emotional – with guitar playing as individuals as well as their sense of what this meant as their experience and expression of female counter-cultural embodiment on stage. Barthes' term *musica practica* sums up the dynamics examined thus far, posited in another of his short pieces of the same name. Published in 1970 Barthes argues that the recorded and professionally performed 'music one listens to [and] the music one plays ... are two totally different arts, each with its own history, its own sociology, its own aesthetics, its own erotic.'[180] For Barthes (any) music that (any)one plays, in non-professionalized spaces above all, constitutes a *practice* that engages the body, experiences (music-making) art as a haptic, sensory act rather than purely auditory, cerebral activity. While Barthes is setting up a rather dichotomous distinction between listening to and playing music, in this reflection he shifts the axis of so-called music appreciation and its long historical and theoretical tail from the mind ('soul') to the embodied agency of music as an activity, a shared practice; a verb rather than an abstract noun that Christopher Small christened 'musicking'.

Barthes' think-piece about the state of the art of music – as a public good – was written at the point that music-as-high-culture was butting up against the cultural and economic inroads of the global market power of the (US owned and controlled) popular culture industries, and just before punk emerged as a countercultural, underground "fuck you" to the slick studio pop and hi-brow classical recording, in turn. As is the case with many continental European thinking on the links between the arts, music, culture and society at this time, in the shadow of Fascism and the Cold War, the figure of Ludwig van Beethoven (1770-1827) enters the discussion. For Barthes, Beethoven epitomizes this historical moment because his work, and how it has become embedded as a western marker of high culture, represents the 'historical problem...the powerful germ of a disturbance of civilization' in play.[181] Recall that as both performer and composer, Beethoven broke the mould, literally (pianos) and mythically (busted open the so-called classical sonata and symphonic form). And while Barthes' conclusions about this titan of 'European Classical Romanticism', a transhistorical icon of music as Great Art, whose music has become also part of popular culture in film and electronic music remixes, are ambivalent, I would argue that Barthes' consideration of the body (some call this *affect*) holds well when considering why punk is more than style, fashion, or marketing genre. Barthes notes, not without melancholy perhaps, that the 'modern location for music is not the concert hall, but the stage on which musicians pass, in what is often a dazzling display from one source of sound to another. It is we who are playing...'.[182] His thinking about *musica practica* in general opens up ways to think about why female punk-bodies, in sonic and physical incarnations, are so formative to punk's countercultural legacy, if not conceit; questions of taste, decorum, or the sex-gender politics of touring being material for another discussion.

Figure 13: Diptych – Kim Gordon and Brix Smith Start
Artist: Mauricio Escobar (all rights reserved)

What has this got to do with punk's sonic and sexual politics of performance (with/out guitar), in the past and in contemporary incarnations? Well, think the sweaty crush of the mosh pit, dancing in the park with others or alone, tapping one's foot, moving the body gently or more vigorously, pogoing or crowd-surfing as opposed to sitting still, not coughing, nodding in quiet, devout appreciation, playing air-keyboard perhaps with the fingers, and so on. Barthes' ideas are helpful for thinking about how punk music "works" as a *musica practica*; namely as:

> 'a *muscular* music in which the part taken by the sense of hearing is one only of ratification, as though the body was hearing ... the body controls, conducts, co-ordinates, having itself to transcribe what it reads, making sound and meaning, the body as inscriber and not just transmitter, simple receiver.'[183]

Whether or not the figure of Beethoven, his "bad boy" attitude and documented "anti-social" behaviour can be considered as a precursor to punk personalities two hundred years later, his musical *praxis* mounted its own sonic challenge to the popular cultural establishment of his time. Considering Beethoven as a 'musician with a future' as Barthes concludes, through the physicality of playing his music, an act of doing rather than of contemplation, is useful for taking punk seriously for how it works as sonic art and performance politics.[184]

Outro

> 'Mostly, I didn't want to be a girl with a guitar. "Girl" felt like an identifier that viewers, especially male ones, saw as a territory upon which an electric guitar was a tourist, an interloper. I wanted the guitar to be an appendage – an extension even – of a body that was made more powerful by my yielding of it. ... I set out from a place where I never assumed that those were acceptable choices or that I could be anything but an accessory to rock 'n' roll. The archetypes, the stage moves, the representations of rebellion and debauchery were all male. ... We wrote and played ourselves right into existence.' (Carrie Brownstein)[185]

> 'I used the guitar to write, but would I say I was a guitar player? No. I didn't think I qualified as a musician. But we were on the brink of punk so, you see, I was in the right place.' (Chrissie Hynde)[186]

There is an underlying ambivalence when the authors write about either (their lack of) any musical qualifications or the many 'guitar-hero' identities pertaining to the proto-punk male personalities or high-profile guitar virtuosi of the time. As women, and as (formerly) novice guitarists, authors delineate between their perceptions of their own playing and what they may (have come to) represent for the shifting sex-gender politics of music-making. As the two passages cited above encapsulate, their circumspection on this – central – topic in the sonography of 20th century pop music is not false modesty, given the unapologetic androcentrism of guitar-playing halls of fame in popular music, and punk publicity's wannabe alter-ego. Hynde, Albertine, Smith Start, Brownstein, and Gordon have all become their own genre of confident guitarist, punk by disposition yet transgressing the strictures of this category from the outset and doing so, it bears repeating, in a predominantly male world. Yet in their overlapping timeframes and narratives of becoming, a reader could also sense how punk as an anti-musical and "amateur" mythos was becoming synonymous with the sonic politics of punk as a *noisy* counterculture.

The uneasy relationship between what scholarship and popular punditry call 'music' and what gets brandished as 'noise' continues since the public furores at the premieres of classical art music's "bad boys." Nonetheless it was and, arguably, still is simply *not done* to connect punk to musicality despite evidence, discussed earlier in Chapter One, to the contrary.[187] As Chrissie Hynde notes on more than one occasion, for proponents of early-generation punk, success and credibility were *not* 'beholden to musicianship. In fact, it was frowned upon if you played too well – that was getting into prog rock territory ... although you weren't supposed to say it, everybody had musical heroes and always had done.'[188] Hynde is particularly astute on this double-standard when she recollects her first meeting with Jimmy Honeyman-Scott (1956-82) with whom she formed the Pretenders:

> 'He particularly disliked punk music, which he didn't find in the slightest bit interesting as it was devoid of musicality and melody. ...We didn't like each other at first... I thought he was too smooth a player and was slightly offended by his total dismissal of punk. ... I still didn't see it. It was clear that Jimmy could play, but I was too blinded by punk to remember how great a great guitar player was.'[189]

Where do these nuances, asides and caveats leave the reader or listener looking, perhaps, to pin "women in punk" down to a clear playlist, ethos, or political affiliation? (In terms of political party preferences there is no direct information apart from what one could infer). A range of emotions and positions are contained in the pages of all these memoirs, experienced along their respective narratives of an author-musician's life. For instance, Kim Gordon writing, in her memoir as well as in a (published) letter she wrote to Karen Carpenter, about how she felt about Carpenter's public unravelling as her illness and unhappiness became apparent: 'She couldn't make peace with her body's curves. ... It was easier for her to disappear; to free herself finally from that body, to find a perfection in dying.'[190] And to Karen herself, Gordon asks; 'who were your role models? ...what's it like being a girl in music?'[191] Or consider how Chrissie Hynde recalls Viv Albertine becoming part of the Slits. In commenting on how Albertine looked at the time Hynde makes a sharp observation about the interplay between gimmick, sexuality, and branding that was an undertow in the punk era as well:

> 'Viv was in a contemplative mood and said, 'Chrissie, the Slits have asked me to be their guitar player'. The Slits were one of the most exciting bands in town... Viv Albertine obviously was the missing link. To add her to the line-up, a buxom blonde, schoolgirl type wearing a crotch-revealing miniskirt would turn the Slits into the kind of band that Russ Meyer would have wanked himself stupid over. Rock and Roll is about gimmicks, after all. Who cares if you're girls or garden gnomes, as long as you've got a sound and the world's attention.'[192]

Hynde's uncensored observation encapsulates the divergent idioms of women writing about making music in this vein and studies of women making music from a range of feminist standpoints that are concerned with the longstanding and unjust invisibility of women in music research and public programming. The 1990s ushered in a school of music scholarship that retrieved forgotten, invisible or misunderstood female composers and performers as part of feminist re-interpretations of the classical musical repertoire, one in which (European) male figures dominate. The memoirists and their stances on topics central to feminist and gender studies thereby become both subjects in and the objects of debates that have unfurled since critical researchers put women, gender and sexuality, along with race and ethnicity, onto university research and teaching agendas. Discovering, or reinserting women into the playlists and scholarship is converging on projects considering the formative role that black and ethnic minority musicians have played in the history of western music. Paying more attention to gender and sexuality as a constitutive factor in music making, as a singular and societal pursuit, has included considerations of multiplex masculinities and femininities, rather than singular essentialist demographics around categories of male and female, where reaching numerical equity remains an aspiration at the societal level. Shifts in focus and emphasis have become part of conducting not only feminist but also critical music research in academe. But such shifts have accompanied concerns about the move from focusing on "women-as-a-group" and thereby moving away from a 'homogeneous approach in gender studies' hat links feminist scholarship directly to women's rights and gender equality advocacy.[193] The historiographical and political dimensions to categorizing feminist research as mutually exclusive periods of political consciousness is a point of critique for music researchers who acknowledge the ongoing need to generate new empirical knowledge and (re)discover not only women but also composers of colour, or from LGBTQ+ communities, so their work can move on to centre-stage in music research and journalism. This is a different, not necessarily antagonistic project to moves in music and other academic research and arts journalism that first put women, as fully-fledged creative agents into musicological analysis and (slowly) on to radio and streaming playlists.

Such debates can be arcane, but they are also political, by definition. They have implications for how the very terms *woman* or *female* can be construed in light of trans-gender awareness and activism that is making an impact in public life, business, and the arts. As Judith Peraino has argued, a shift from feminist research focusing on women as a demographic category fosters a 'pragmatic and postmodern approach to gender, and, in reaction to the sexual conservatism of many second-wave feminists, is particularly concerned with sexuality'. Peraino welcomes the link between how music industry publications began to address imbalance towards women's role in popular music in the 1980s and 1990s and the arrival of 'third wave feminism' with its 'very rock 'n' roll sensibility' about sex and gender, in everyday life and public institutions.[194] But Peraino's approval is not unmitigated; when looking to redress the *relative* neglect of women in music research, or considering women as a minority group in the music industry, or high-profile female artists who make it against the odds, another set of sex-gender stereotypes become ingrained; women in music as outsiders, misfits, "bad girls." extraordinary. Memoirists like Albertine and Gordon often articulate their careers, their creative journeys in retrospective, as the achievements of 'typical girls'. With these analytical hazards in mind I would agree with Peraino when she considers what could be revealed by moving up 'to the next level of inquiry: how rock is a discursive practice of gender and sexuality such that women are constituted as "trouble"'.[195] This insight is invaluable for considering the overlaps, and contradictions about not just what it means to be a 'girl in a band', 'woman with guitar', or 'she-punk' in general but what it means for the subject, the musician who is playing.

Our musician-memoirists provide multiple insights into how they experienced, in their own bodies and through performance, making music their own way, without referring to either Barthes or Beethoven, Butler or Connell. They consider punk-musicmaking as an aspect of other creative work, in light of which albums, songs worked better than others, why some albums could have been better or worse, how their creative practices have developed with time. Authors also discuss their emotional attachments to (first and successive) guitars as compositional and induction vehicles for aspiring performers without formal musical training. The importance of the (bass) guitar riff and unpolished playing style are also key points of technique, identity, and pride, as is the joy of creating something from scratch without the usual technical skillset.

5. VANGUARD OR OLD GUARD?

Hip Priestess: Coat, Skirt, Hair, Hat

> 'This woman is not for resigning!' (Pauline Black)[196]

Authors, from around the punk compass of countercultural pop-rock performance values, articulate different sensibilities about "look." on stage and elsewhere, across the memoir-set. These distinctions have implications for how readers might engage with the authors' recollections as a cumulative public archive of first-hand accounts of music making in which women are the main act. They also articulate the contours of career-paths, self-chosen and fortuitous, as authors move in and out of music-making through other cultural domains. Take three examples: first Brix Smith Start, who in her life and career after leaving the Fall – and Mark E. Smith – went on to open the shop START in London's Shoreditch, which took her onto popular British television in the 2000s, as stylist alongside TV everyday-style guru Gok Wan in his show *Gok's Fashion Fix*.[197] Smith Start's observation about fashion and 'style' in the wake of punk's initial decades underscores her longstanding interest in popular cultural iconography (e.g. she writes of her love for Disney's Mickey Mouse) and awareness of the influential representational impulse that drives popular media and entertainment as public audiovisual culture:

> 'The lens of a camera is like a powerful opinionated eye. It sees things in its own way. To be a great television stylist you have to study the image of the garment on the monitor, not with the naked eye. To be a great TV stylist you first have to see through the eyes of the TV.'[198]

Chrissie Hynde, for her part, highlights how punk fashion, as haute couture, not only propelled but also, for some critics, undercut the public profile of the DIY ethos that has become associated with first-generation punk. Like Viv Albertine, Hynde devotes some pages to her time working in the Vivienne Westwood and Malcolm McLaren shop SEX on the King's Road, the epicentre of British 1970s punk's burgeoning fashion and music scenes, and meeting-point for a number of punk's emerging celebrities at the time. Hynde recalls that, counter to punk from a musicological point of view:

> 'It was all about the clothes; the clothes did the talking. ... Nobody I knew thought about fashion. Designer labels didn't exist, not to people like us anyway. Gucci? That was for someone's sad auntie. But being around Malcolm {McLaren} and Viv {Westwood}, I started to understand the meaning of glamour: that how you present yourself to your fellow man is a way of communicating ideas.'[199]

What we can perceive more clearly in first-hand recollections from the Albertine, Hagen, and Hynde memoirs is the prominence of Vivienne Westwood, as a female role model. Appraisals of the part Westwood, who died on December 29, 2022 at the age of 81, played in the durability of punk as a *polyglot* sartorial and embodied creative practice can now begin. The fondness with which Hynde, Albertine and others recall their time in Westwood's orbit, acknowledging her influence on their sense of punk styling, is in contrast to the lack of attention to Westwood's role in obituaries following the death of Malcolm McLaren, her former business and life-partner- and Sex Pistols manager – who died over a decade before her.

And, third, a Cosey Fanni Tutti recollection from quite another point on the DIY aesthetic compass:

> '"The COUMing of Age" show at the Oval House Theatre in London {in 1974} was the first COUM action that involved nudity ... The show was an odd collection of innocent, clichéd sexual fantasies and scenarios – but with twists. We took the sugary-sweet image of a virgin-like girl on a swing revealing brief glimpses of her knickers as her skirt blew in the wind and presented me naked on a pale-pink swing hung centre-stage from the theatre ceiling ... as I pushed higher and higher to send me over the audience, I peed through the heart-shaped hole we'd cut in the seat, releasing an arc of warm wetness as I swung back and forth, slowly coming to a dribbling standstill.'[200]

Such episodes from Cosey's time with her early collectives, COUM and Throbbing Gristle, sets her oeuvre and public persona somewhat apart from the other memoirists. Explicitly sexualised displays as part of live shows that deployed a combination of DIY viscerality and iconoclasm were core elements to the Throbbing Gristle sonic and visual repertoire. Sexuality and intimate relationships, some painful and others bitter-sweet are present in the other memoirs, but sex – as work and pleasure – as a bodily function and creative channel is not discussed as up-front as they are in the two Cosey memoirs: Viv Albertine is one exception as she provides graphic descriptions of being constipated, what turns her on, or a violent altercation with her sister at their mother's deathbed. But these moments are part of Albertine's personal life, not her aesthetic. The differences in "writing dirty." are germane to how readers might also assess the authors' contribution to punk's challenge to public mores in terms of what they reveal about their private lives and public profiles, at the time and in retrospect; Patti Smith's retreat from performing – to live in the countryside and raise a family with her husband – before re-emerging on the live concert circuit in the 1990s comes to mind, as does Viv Albertine's account of her 'suburban housewife' period between her time with the Slits and return to public performance and the music studio. Kim Gordon combines life on the road and burgeoning creative projects with family life, as do Cosey and Hynde while Pauline Black recounts the pressure that life on the road had on her marriage. The lifepaths and personal struggles presented are recognizable, for some readers perhaps all too recognizable, not 'extraordinary' or 'alternative' enough.[201]

Cosey, on the other hand, has made a career and a living through personifying her expression of anti-establishment attitudes to sex, monogamy, and mainstream creative practice through the part she played in setting up and sustaining the COUM/Throbbing Gristle projects and eventually the electronic industrial route that she claims as her own, alongside partner Chris Carter. In her writing on her own work and life Cosey is the most explicit about sex as a private act and public art, including her time working in the sex industry and the material she took from this period to shape into artworks. The double standard with which her various public expressions of naked embodiments through commercial sexual tropes has been treated in the press is a refrain to which Cosey often returns, in both memoirs. Her body of work remains controversial to this day for pundits, and some schools of women's rights activism. Cosey is mindful in both memoirs to mark the distinction between her (shared with collectives past and present) back catalogues, sonic and visual, and punk's hegemonic discourse of masculinised working-class antiheroes and their female counterparts.

The line Cosey draws here is because she does not identify with the punk counter-aesthetic, nor the historical circumstances that saw her time with Throbbing Gristle overlapping the first generation of British punk bands as they, too, exploited a DIY aesthetic and approach to independent recording and marketing. There is no love lost between Cosey in her sense of anti-establishment subjectivity and creative drive and the putative 'punk royalty' label afforded to the Slits and contemporaneous bands. For instance, Cosey recalls some 'of the girls from the punk bands the Slits and the Raincoats' being drunk at a Throbbing Gristle gig in London who, she recalls, went on to 'attack the stage, trying to unplug the equipment, throwing bottles and glasses at us... One of the Slits came over to me, trying to provoke me, saying she thought I was cool but now thought I was shit ... I didn't give a toss what she thought of me ... and I wasn't interested in having a conversation with a drunk.'²⁰² Across the memoir-set there are few accounts of confrontations such as this 'live'. The Throbbing Gristle DIY aesthetic and no-holds barred approach to subverting the slick pop music production model also represents punk's countercultural conceit, if not entirely its power-chord sonics, or its safety-pin, mohawk, Doc Martin sartorial style now preserved in photographic and video archives. For this reason, the two Cosey Fanni Tutti memoirs are included in this study even as the author is fashioning her past life and work as beyond the purview of punkography. Carrie Brownstein makes a comparable distinction between her sense of Sleater-Kinney and the riot grrrl feminist political scene with which they are associated.

Figure 14: Patti Smith
Artist: Mauricio Escobar (all rights reserved)

The memoirs written by women born before the turn of this century, about a musico-cultural moment that took off decades ago begs the question of whether what they are talking about, and how they present their creative and personal lives add anything to knowledge. Are the authors "vanguard" or "old guard?" Do their accounts of punk as *music* making *politics* offer younger generations of women something to take with them through their own journeys, as individuals and communities? The answer to such questions lies with emerging generations of researchers and artists. At the very least the memoir-set provides a substantial empirical and autobiographical contribution to changing the default settings for work on how successive *mediascapes* and their respective cultural industries are integral elements in society and politics. With this claim in mind, the chapter considers such extra-musical themes as they "present" in the memoirs when authors consider their experience of both public appreciation and disapproval of how they – as women – (should) behave, dress, and sound in public. How academic and industry pundits respond to the memoirs, or their authors as individuals or archetypes, also plays a role in whether the rock *femoir* will ever get taken as seriously as the rock *manmoir*. Commenting on critical receptions of the first wave of memoirs studied here, journalist Kaitlin Fontana observes that the issues are less about whether or not a female memoirist 'reveals all' (none of them do, even Cosey for all her frankness) but, rather how such accounts throw into relief 'hegemonic discourses' about stardom, creativity, performance as a cultural achievement. Fontana observes how 'this duality – bad girl vs. good girl – points to larger, more pervasive problems to do with how women are viewed in culture.'[203]

'Punk and Poses'[204]

That being preoccupied with approval for how one looks is an innately 'feminine' pursuit is a cliché batted away since the gender-defying apparel of glam/rock/new-wave male headliners such as Marc Bolan, David Bowie, the New York Dolls, Boy George or, in recent years, Sam Smith for instance. Male punk rockers recuperated a certain (shabby) male chic by way of the ripped t-shirt, grubby jeans, and Doc Martin footwear outfits in bands like the Sex Pistols. Female punks followed suit up to a point. But generalizations like these underscore the prevalence of high-profile personalities in the public media rather than their empirical veracity. Women in these years played a formative role in a gamut of sartorial gestures that challenge sex-gender stereotyping in industry-branding of women in music as much as they have stretched such stereotypes beyond recognition; underwear as outer-wear, degrees of public nudity, if not on-stage undress that rival those of Iggy Pop or Sid Vicious for instance, or repurposed men's wear such as jackets, hats, and shirts. Research into the politics of fashion and popular culture include scholarship on punk fashion as a particular moment in the evolution of popular *style*; from its hair-dos and surfeit of safety-pins, to the deployment of clothing items from bondage and S&M scenes, and (controversially) Nazi regalia, which featured in the lines that Vivienne Westwood designed for SEX. How punk looked in its heyday was also down to punk's historical catalogue of larger-than-life personalities) who would nowadays be tagged as media celebrities, such as Jordan (b. Pamela Rooke, 1955-2022) or Siouxsie Sioux (one time groupie and then lead vocalist in her own band), all of whom had a part to play in the visual imaginaries of punk's sonic idioms.[205]

Look, therefore, that is, sartorial inflections and fashioned embodiments in the narratives, bears some of our attention: Not only on what clothes to wear but also on how working on, or against a particular 'look' was part of learning the ropes, on one's own terms. Buying or acquiring second-hand clothes entailed substantial investment as is the case for Viv Albertine. Particular items of dress become recurring points of chronological and emotional reference for Patti Smith and in the case of Brix Smith Start fashion and styling lead into a future career-path. For Pauline Black fashioning her own 2-tone wardrobe is an avenue for her coming to terms with her mixed-race heritage and engagement with anti-racism mobilization in 1970s and 1980s UK.

Patti Smith's memoir writing is punctuated with references to particular items of clothing, as signifiers of subjective intimacy: shoes, coats, hats, and accessories; her own and those of others such as her late husband, friends, lovers. In her writing items of clothing denote a person, a gesture, a memory, literary hooks that serve as refrains in subsequent memoirs as she recalls last meetings, memories, and dreams – of Sam Shepard, Sandy Pearlman, or Fred Smith. With a sense of irony (that she seldom deploys), Smith recalls, in *Just Kids* with some precision not only how others she mixed with in the early years (orbiting around the Chelsea Hotel in mid-Manhattan, and Greenwich Village) dressed but also how she regarded this ritual in her relationship with Robert Mapplethorpe, during his coming-out as a gay man:

> 'I [Smith] approached dressing like an extra preparing for a shot in a French New Wave film. I had a few looks, such as a striped boatneck shirt and a red throat scarf like Yves Montand in *Wages of Fear*, a Left Bank beat look with green tights and red ballet slippers, or my take on Audrey Hepburn in Funny Face, with her long black sweater, black tights, white socks, and black Capezios. Whatever the scenario, I usually needed about ten minutes to get ready.
>
> Robert [Mapplethorpe] approached dressing like living art. ... Waiting as Robert decided on the right number of keys to hand on his belt loop was humorously maddening....Finally the moment would arrive to tackle the Shakespearean question: should he or should he not wear three necklaces?'[206]

In voice, and visually as an embodiment of female androgyny Smith was path-breaking at the time as well, on stage and in everyday terms as she sported T-Shirts, black jackets and ties in one variation and, in another, under-over forms of dressiness, such as camisoles, complete with unshaved armpits.[207] Smith writes of being aware of her emerging image as androgynous that included her sporting a Keith Richard haircut, one of the many signals in Smith's memoirizing of her own music-fan affiliations. Shaw in his study of the *Horses* album notes how Smith's anti-fashion show interventions worked in tandem with her early live performances, and ground-breaking imago. Both these looks, cross-dresser and subverted nymph, are immortalized in the portraits for the album covers of *Horses* and the second album, *Easter* (1978), photographs from Robert Mapplethorpe and Lynn Goldsmith respectively. Onstage, at least in the video archives from her first period (the 1970s), Smith wears jeans and a t-shirt; the latter being one of her go-to items when packing her bags. Watching Smith in these earlier videos, but also in later years, offers a visual clue to her status as 'godmother of punk' even when, musically, she considers herself to be a 'rock 'n' roll' musician, and performance-wise the instigator of 'Rock 'n' Rimbaud', namely performances in which Smith curated a broad repertoire of 'poems and songs revolving around [her] love of Rimbaud'; an engagement with the generation of surrealist French poets that she continues to explore to this day.[208]

The sartorial inflections that the memoirists brought to their public personae as novice punks initially pushed back against the ways in which recording companies looked to craft female artists, at least before 'punk' itself entered the stylist's lexicon. Grooming within commercial music's marketing strategies is an approach that the dominant American labels perfected, for instance Motown records which perfected a look as well as a sound for its artists; an aspect to the grooming of Black women in the mid-twentieth century music industry that Danyel Smith critiques in her 'very personal' case-studies of high-profile Black women in American popular music.[209] Pauline Black's accounts of her hair – cultivating an Afro, the clothes for the 'rude girl' look she worked on for the Selecter's public imaging, and hats form a refrain through her memoir, *Black by Design*. Black's memoir pivots on her growing up in Coventry as the adopted 'half-caste ... coloured' child of white parents and coming of age through her encounter with Jamaican reggae and ska musicians as the Selecter took its place at the epicentre of the ska/2-tone scene emerging alongside those of early UK punk, both of which took part in the anti-racism musico-activism of 1980s Thatcherite Britain:

> 'The sight of this proud black woman [Aretha Franklin performing 'Respect' on the BBC TV program, *Top of the Pops*], with her unprocessed hair in a natural Afro, walking down the street like a modern-day African Queen, singing such a simple powerful truth, made my heart swell with pride – this new black pride that was increasingly being talked about. ...Until then it had never occurred to me that how I wore my hair was a political decision.'[210]

Black recounts the impact of her Afro at home with her white family and in school, as she took her distance from the 'processed hair' characterizing the look of Motown stars such as Diana Ross and the Supremes and made visible her increasing political awareness of race politics:

> 'My Afro was huge. Look at me, the Afro screamed, as it bobbed along on my head, oblivious to the stares of passers-by; it was as if it had a life of its own. It was wearing me, not the other way around. It bounced contentedly while surveying the world from a lofty height and, by comparison with its very hipness, everything else looked outdated, outmoded and, dare I say it, plain lame.'[211]

Black's reconstruction of the outfit she crafted and its political significance for the ska bands who emerged as part of first-wave punk bands in the UK offers valuable insights into the race-class-gender contours for women in punkographies who were from mixed race and working class backgrounds, Black, and Poly Styrene (from X-Ray Spex), led the way in this regard. Settling on a look that worked for her and also represented the Selecter as a fully-fledged 2-tone band took Black to second-hand shops (a popular source for many a DIY, improvised punk look at the time). But the second-hand shop approach to what-to-wear was not self-explanatory for other members of the Selecter:

> 'Caribbean people don't like wearing other people's cast-offs. They want to buy new clothes with their money, not clothes that other people don't want any more, or worse, 'dead man's threads'. That's why hip-hop artists dress themselves in designer stuff and bling. Black people don't want to look poor, as though they haven't got the money for store-bought clothes.'[212]

Figure 15: Pauline Black (with hat)
Artist: Mauricio Escobar (all rights reserved)

Black notes she was less concerned with this discomfort than with settling on the right look; opting for 'the "rude boy" look that Peter Tosh had pioneered in his early ska days and feminized it'. In so doing Black writes that they 'decided that my Afro hair did not suit this ensemble, so I pulled it up into a small topknot. I felt curiously empowered when I tried the clothes on at home and surveyed the result in the bathroom mirror'. The finishing touch was her, by now, trademark hat, 'a dove-grey fedora with a dark grey ribbon hatband. As soon as I tried it on, I felt perfectly attired.'[213]

These passages highlight an under-researched dimension to punkographies, the complex *intersection* of race, class, and gender sensibilities for individual musicians, their bands, and their fans, which do not necessarily work in sync. Black is writing about coming to terms with her own intersectionality of race, gender, and class as she recreates herself, including her name and persona as 'black by design'. As is the case with other memoirists, the punk era aesthetic with its multiple wardrobes was not a monolithic 'style'. The high-profile presence, and musical influence of ska and 2-tone bands in this same time period worked, and sounded across crisscrossing strands of identification and signification, for musicians and their publics, producers and concert promoters. For instance; the presence of skinheads identifying with extreme right-wing, racist nationalist politics in punk concerts, making their presence felt in 2-tone gigs as well, is an undercurrent in the history of punk as the music made for, and by left-leaning exponents and their fans. Pauline Black writes of incidents during Selecter events in which racial (and sexist) abuse by skinhead contingents made live performance dangerous in ways that contrast to the bust-ups and confrontations between punk acts and their audiences. In a different vein, Viv Albertine provides a comprehensive index on the first of the three themes in her book title (clothes, clothes, clothes), a tongue-in-cheek concession to curious readers looking for gossip on sex, drugs, and rock 'n' roll as she quotes her mother. These quick-reference guides are at the front, and back ends of the book and they provide a rich vein of inquiry in their own right for clothes, subculture styles at the time, and music. Chrissie Hynde was definitely impressed at the time she recalls (see Chapter Four)[214]. Nina Hagen writes for her part of being inspired by the look that Ari Up and Albertine made the hallmark of the Slits.[215]

The album cover of *Cut*, the first and most influential album from the Slits (in its first iteration as the band was to have several line-ups) pictures the three band members topless, in improvised grass skirts and covered in mud.[216] The photo, controversial even more nowadays perhaps, countermands that of Patti Smith yet also conjoins her visual repertoire for their shared refusal to be depicted as "pretty little things." Nina Hagen makes this point in no uncertain terms; punk was more than a fad, not reducible to a fashion trend in her eyes. And it was much more than an Anglo-American androcentric invention. As far as Hagen is concerned, she was a punk already, growing up in the former East Germany, living and working with counter-cultural figures there who looked towards the Anglo-American pop music trends but who created their own versions of both main/malestream and underground pop-rock-punk music. Punk in this reading was, then, as much about pushing back against capitalist commercialism as it was about contesting what Hagen calls the 'Stalinist Conformist Machine.'[217]

Race-Gender-Class Horizons

There are any number of empirical and conceptual permutations when considering how the authors recollect their encounters with sexism, exploitation, poverty, violence, or racism in the case of Black and Alice Bag in particular. As introduced earlier, the analytical concept, *intersectionality* serves as a rubric for unpacking such dynamics in terms of how they can be seen at work, measured and observed, through the lived experience of individuals but also calcified, structural relationships of unequal opportunity, discrimination, or educational achievement. The term, coined by legal scholar Kimberlé Crenshaw in the late 1980s, is also evoked when considering the converse, how privilege and opportunity work for some sectors of society more than others. Other dimensions have since been included in the burgeoning fields of intersectionality studies, feminism, and critical race theory such as caste, religion, disability as these contribute to what Crenshaw' calls 'multiple oppressions'. While the memoirists do not explicitly engage these debates, the intersections that Crenshaw and generations of activists and scholars have been bringing to light are present between the lines; namely, as Patricia Hill Collins and Sirma Bilge stipulate, the notion of intersectionality encapsulates how 'in a given society at a given time, power relations of race, class, and gender, for example, are not discrete and mutually exclusive entities but rather build on each other and work together... while often invisible....'.[218] Pauline Black encapsulates one moment that serves as an illustration when she writes about realizing that 'how I wore my hair was a political decision' as a mixed-race woman growing up in 1960s and 1970s Britain where it was 'as if black people didn't exist on the high street and, in terms of spending power, they didn't.'[219]

Sex-Gender

Back to Cosey and her reflections on her engagements with sex work as an artistic undertaking; These insights shift in tone and detail from the first memoir to her second book in which she weaves her work and life after Throbbing Gristle with her interest in the lives of British electronic composer, Delia Derbyshire (1937-2001) and Middle Age mystic, Margery Kempe. Cosey, looking back as she curates a retrospective in her first memoir, is still nonplussed at the ongoing controversy around some of her chosen exhibits, decades after their first public airing:

> '(W)e had established (via the Tate and other institutions) the magazines were art and not pornographic. They were my art-sex actions, and as such their presentation in a gallery resisted their original context. That was key to the concept of the magazine actions. It seemed acceptable for Jeff Kroons to do a hard-core pastiche like 'Made in Heaven' using the porn star Ciccolina and her reputation, but as a female artist who revealed all, my work was still a problem.'[220]

There is a rich vein of inquiry to be had on Cosey's presentation of her creative work and life-path as art, sex and music, the title of the first memoir, for what it can offer debates on both the sex-gender politics of the memoir-writing business and the agenda-setting power of arts curatorship. But for the purposes of this discussion I will focus on selected passages in her own words: Cosey is clear of the role that her work with COUM and Throbbing Gristle has had on her artistic sensibility from the outset: the 'COUM shows were a hybrid of art and music, with an increasing emphasis on extreme and obscure actions' she recalls about the convergence between the COUM/Throbbing Gristle collectives and the visual performative aesthetic of sex work.[221] She writes about dealing with the discomfort of 'getting naked with people you've never met before, let alone having sex with them in front of a camera crew and lighting technicians, but I adjusted to it... I dealt with it by looking at it as a job, disengaging from emotion ... There was no pleasure, love or desire involved; it was simply job-descriptive sex – that in itself was a revelation to me.'[222]

Engaging with sex-work as a fully immersed participant-observer brought with it its own hazards, about which Cosey is unflinching in her account as she considers she entered this domain as an artist conducting research, not a professional practitioner. She notes how 'the models I worked with didn't know the reason behind my doing modelling and porn' acknowledging her relatively privileged position vis-à-vis the diverse reasons others were working in the business while also noting that as she gains experience working 'with familiar faces made life much easier'. Cosey's reflection on what she learned in this period is couched in her life-motto, one that is reiterated throughout the second memoir, and its dedication, '*self*hood': 'Relinquishing control of my image and identity was an important part of the project, and that intrigued me as much as the experience of the process of co-creating those images.'[223]

Race-Class

'Oh Bondage, Up Yours!' (Poly Styrene)

'Acceptance and identification are two different things.' (Pauline Black)[224]

'Oh Bondage, up yours!' is the title line of the X-Ray Spex single from 1977. Their lead vocalist, Poly Styrene, delivers these lines at the top of her voice, and vocal register. Born Marianne Elliot-Said (1957-2011), of Scottish, Irish and Somali descent, Poly Styrene during her punk days was based in Brixton, south London and this track has come to epitomize the sexual politics of women in punk. With books, films, and documentaries about protagonists in the multilayered narrative of punk accumulating, the life story and creative impulses of Poly Styrene in her own words will never get published. She died young, of cancer, as did Ari

Up of the Slits. At the risk of belabouring the point, the reference to bondage is figurative, and literal as Vivienne Westwood's punk fashion aesthetic exploited the paraphernalia of S&M Bondage scenes. In another register, sartorially and personally, Pauline Black, for her part, took very seriously the link between race politics, music making and look, decisions about which that have implications for a band's perceived "authenticity."

> 'I was stuck in the middle, that miserable "between a rock and a hard place" void, where most mixed-race people find themselves from time to time. I'd always wanted to promote my black credentials, but these seemed very different from Jamaican credentials. ... I was in love with the illusion of Angela Davis and the Black Panthers. I was dancing to a Black American aesthetic, not a Jamaican one, even if I was the lead singer in a band that did Jamaican music. I was confused.'[225]

The uneasy relationship between popular music as an industry, with punk as its putative alter ego, and women's rights activism rumbles between the lines in the memoir-set. Cosey Fanni Tutti and Pauline Black are direct about how they encountered feminist critiques of their participation in public culture of the 1970s and 1980s. Cosey has not forgotten how the British feminist magazine, *Spare Rib*, 'gave me such as hard time about my sex magazine art project in the *Prostitution* exhibition' at the ICA in London, an event that was shut down after public outcry. Black notes the presence of the 'boiler-suited and monkey-booted feminist movement...making itself heard in Britain for the first time, much to the chagrin of Britain's as yet unreconstructed men. Some of these ladies also beat a path to the door of the 2-Tone movement.'[226]

"I'm not a Feminist"

For women who made their names as punk musicians or have become identified as such as the term has become more elastic over time, and whose memoirs feature in this study, the feminist label was, and still is not self-explanatory. How the authors reflect on how they dressed or perceive themselves performing on-stage resonates with ongoing discomforts and ideological rifts about what the form and substance of feminism as a political movement and scholarly specialism.[227] Chrissie Hynde, characteristically, makes a bold assertion on all counts:

> 'No. I didn't think I qualified as a musician. But we were on the brink of punk so, you see, I was in the right place. ... How I fit in that scenario I had no idea. It would have to be something that transcended gender. Rock was masculine but its listeners were feminine. It was never gender-restrictive – men loved to see a woman play a guitar; they always had. I'd have to figure it out as I didn't want to be a waitress again.'[228]

Considering *intersectionality* as an empirical and analytical device helps to keep at the forefront the complex sociocultural relationships of making music, or any art for that matter, along with their political and economic underpinnings.

Figure 16: Chrissie Hynde
Artist: Mauricio Escobar (all rights reserved)

As a cluster of memoirs, authors are revealing their own lives including their attitudes towards feminist politics, racism, and social movements. They are not writing academic research or political manifestos. Memory does not work along a script nor does it offer cosy labels by which to categorize or judge the author's contribution, to art, politics, society and so on. Hynde in the recollection cited above about the link between (masculinized) sex and (male) music stardom is making an acerbic observation with the benefit of hindsight, and as someone who has had success as a female guitarist in a male-dominated field. In this narrative arc, waitressing epitomizes 'before': Neither did Brix Smith Start want to be a waitress again despite doing just that between her time with the Fall, and her subsequent career and life partners.[229] As for Cosey, given her engagement with the sex industry as part of her creative projects when with Throbbing Gristle, such recollections cannot be so easily tossed off. She writes:

> 'Retrieving my COUM and magazine works [in 2000] from the boxes in the archive room was like delving into a past that I'd been very happy to leave behind. ... Flicking through the pages of the magazines triggered a myriad of emotions and memories ... brought back the events hidden behind the procuring of that final printed image. But the shock wasn't that, nor the graphic detail of crotch shots, but just how much these magazines were a rich visual time capsule of the blatant 1970s

sexism that I'd lived through, coped with, and which now looked ridiculous, sometimes shocking and crass ... Those works have since been presented within a "feminist" context and I can now appreciate why, but for me at the time (and always) it was about my freedom to be me not about "feminism" per se.'[230]

Cosey is even more condemnatory in the second memoir which chronicles her burgeoning list of art gallery retrospectives and work on a film about electronic music pioneer Delia Derbyshire with actor and film maker Caroline Catz. But this was also the period in which, according to Cosey herself, she was being subjected to sexual abuse and emotional coercion by her former partner and collaborator, Genesis P-Orridge.[231] She is consistent on her antagonism towards Second Wave feminist platforms in light of public criticism of her sex-artwork:

'As a willing participant [in the sex industry] I'd placed myself in a position to be used this way, and right in the line of fire of 1970s feminism. The sexual exploitation and objectification of women by men was the feminist hot topic ... and I and other sex workers were perceived as the enemy. I didn't identify with 1970s feminism: it didn't speak for me or the diverse and complex nature of women. I was a free spirit and didn't want more rules and guilt thrown at me about my actions. ...I was no "victim" of exploitation. I was exploiting the sex industry for my own purposes, to subvert and use it to create my own art.'[232]

Tensions, between activists' condemnation of porn as patriarchy and sexism exemplified on the one hand and, on the other, debates about the civil liberties implication of arts censorship, is a line of continuity in both of Cosey's memoirs. In the second, as she embarks on a series of retrospectives in galleries around Europe and takes her place as a sought-after cultural icon in high-profile art events Cosey underscores the ongoing unease, in both high-art and popular culture domains, with (full) female nudity or explicit sexuality. She highlights a strand of conservatism within Anglo-American feminist movements, and successive generations whose primary objective is combating sexual violence against women, human trafficking, and pornography as oppressive for all women. The arguments rage on today as activists and scholars line up on either side of this ideological divide between feminism as a political movement for structural change or one in which individual agency, choice, is the goal. As her 'I am not a feminist' credentials become public record, Cosey's libertarian ethos, one that rejects political orthodoxies is, nonetheless, attune to the unconscious bias, the favouritism that the 'commercial and "fine art" worlds' display towards male artists. Her work, and that of other women in this domain, has been 'either shunned.....or criticised because of the sexual content of our work, our use of our naked bodies, our sexualised performances and, in my case, exploring and taking part in pornography as part of my art practice.'²³³ Later in her life, being 'accused of being anti-feminist' yet also 'hailed as a feminist for asserting my autonomy in forging my path to freedom of expression, claiming my body as my own and my right to choose what to do with it' simply confirms Cosey's self-perception as an 'outsider' even as the artworld has come to consider her work as "art" (the scare quotes are hers) and in so doing 'leaving the integrity of my work uncompromised.'²³⁴

From another generational vantage point, Carrie Brownstein, who came of age in the 1990s during the shift from Second Wave to Third Wave feminism (discussed in Chapter Four) does identify as feminist and the public political stance that ensues. Yet she also takes issue with the riot grrrl 'brand' of music making as a particular codification of subverted femininized embodiments.²³⁵ It would be hasty, however, to reduce such statements to ego-politics or in-fighting; not that such dynamics are absent in the narratives. For instance, those groups defined as punk's contribution to the history of 'girl bands', the Slits and Sleater-Kinney in particular, personalities had a role to play. Albertine does not pull any punches here in how she recalls her clashes with equally strong characters in the group, lead singer Ari Up in particular or arrogant, opinionated sound technicians, publicists and managers.²³⁶ Brownstein's memoir is all about Sleater-Kinney as an emotional and ferociously original force.²³⁷ She writes a lot about their 'habit of meta-songwriting, where we were in a band writing about being in a band, singing about singing.'²³⁸ This is also the case for Kim Gordon in her recounting of life as 'the (ex-)wife of, 'girl' bass-player, and all the while co-creator of much of Sonic Youth's output.'

In Brownstein's case, the first-person narrative voice shifts up a gear when considering the relationship between Sleater-Kinney's internal musical and personality politics on the one hand and, on the other, feminism and social justice mobilization in the 1990s. For instance, in *Hunger Makes Me a Modern Girl*, close to the halfway point in the book the author takes leave of the chronological (career) narrative to make a musico-political statement. In this chapter (Chapter 8, 'Call the Doctor', named after the band's second album) Brownstein reflects on how Sleater-Kinney started out unwittingly as a 'girl band' positioned as part of the riot grrrl feminist punk rock scenes in the northwest of the US.²³⁹ Maintaining their own creative path through these times meant side-stepping the industry's tendency, once a band has been "discovered." to pigeon-hole the music for programmatic, and marketing purposes:

> '[P]eople were staking out territory, constructing niches in a punk landscape that felt vast. Parcelled out like land claims, punk [in the US] was divided by city, by sound, and indexers like gender and sexual orientation. ... Much of it boiled down to identity, a way of differentiating punk from the rest of the world, making it subversive, confrontational. Whether quiet or loud, fast or slow, pretty or ugly – it was

not about a sound or a look – punk was about making choices that didn't bend to consumptive and consumerist inclinations and ideologies, that didn't commodify the music or ourselves. We [Sleater-Kinney] didn't want to be associated with a brand. Mostly, we didn't want to be a brand. There was no middle ground.'[240]

Brownstein is also writing in this chapter on the inception and development of the band itself in terms of how she and Corin Tucker (co-writer, vocalist and guitar) collaborated musically, intuitively and 'amateurishly' as the founding core of Sleater-Kinney, yet aware of others' influence on how they would come to perceive the music-work: from male stars of US punk, such as Joey Ramone from The Ramones – 'a performer who embodied both gawkiness and grandiosity' – to Donna Dresch and her 'queercore' band, Team Dresch.[241] Pearson in his study of US hardcore scenes in the UK briefly considers female punk bands, noting the complexities of the feminist politics that bands under the riot grrrls rubric expressed in interviews, as a real-life politics and for their on-stage personae.[242] What is most striking about how feminist issues are rendered in much research literature is the sense of surprise that feminism, as is the case where any social movement overlaps scholarly and public culture discussions, might be complex, a constellation of often quite opposing points of view about what needs to be done, where, when, and by whom.

Since – On Getting Younger

'There comes a time, whether you like it or not, your body tells you to slow down. Much as everyone hates that moment, it's a reality we all face. ... The schedules for playing live can be unforgivingly physically demanding. Trouble is, there's nothing that can compare with when you're on stage, lost in the magic of music with an audience that is with you all the way.' (Cosey Fanni Tutti)[243]

'I have this theory that many women in the media spotlight reach an age – usually somewhere between forty-five and fifty-five as the menopause beckons – when the powers-that-be, rather undiplomatically, reckon that their faces are now more suited to radio. ... Very few women in music, TV or film are allowed or perhaps are prepared to show everybody how a woman looks at a certain age, but so many men, Mick Jagger, Ronnie Wood, Rod Stewart and Clint Eastwood, to name but a few, are allowed to wrinkle or sag with impunity.' (Pauline Black)[244]

5. VANGUARD OR OLD GUARD?   111

Figure 17: Pauline Black
Artist: Mauricio Escobar (all rights reserved)

At the outset I considered studies of women's music memoirs that put the stress on getting older as a primary catalyst for a woman undertaking a memoir. The feminist premise of 'taking back' the menopause from its pejorative connotations has provided one avenue of exploration in this regard. The authors are less preoccupied with their biological clocks as a signifier of decay, or discrimination; their life stories are packed with how they encountered sexism, gender-based violence, and contempt from mainstream cultural institutions from an early age. That said, neither is aging avoided in the memoirs. It is treated as the passing of time, as mortal lives when loved ones pass away – a leitmotiv for Patti Smith in particular. Getting older is not granted a headline role in the memoirs even as the authors express their own, personal experiences of ageism. Cosey acknowledges the toll on the body of live concert performances and touring in the passage above. Pauline Black, towards the end of her memoir is frank in her condemnation of the ongoing double-standard for women in public life, in the arts and entertainment industries especially. Black's observation cited above is neither idle nor a conceited comment in light of evidence of the structural ageism that pervades public broadcasting worldwide.

Since their formative years our memoirists have continued to create music across a number of industry marketing genres, their punk pedigree more or less intact. They have released solo albums in recent years (Viv Albertine, Alice Bag, Kim Gordon, Brix Smith Start), written other books, scored soundtracks for films and ballet – Cosey Fanni Tutti and Kim Gordon respectively – and diversified their musical repertoire in various post-punk formations that include tributes to other women musical pioneers; such as Nico (Patti Smith, and Cosey Fanni Tutti), blues and jazz (Chrissie Hynde), and Delia Derbyshire (Cosey Fanni Tutti). Others have got into television, fashion shows (Smith Start), satirical comedy such as *Portlandia* (Brownstein), and theatre (Black). Several have gained tertiary qualifications (Bag, Black, Albertine, and Cosey) along with public honours; Pauline Black was awarded an OBE (Order of the British Empire) in 2022 for services to entertainment, Patti Smith is the holder of several honorary doctorates, from Columbia University (2022) and Wesleyan University (2016) to name but two. They have had families, reunited with former bandmates and started touring again, found, lost and found again the various spiritual paths that are intertwined with their personal timelines and forays into public culture through the opportunities that punk presented to newcomers.

While authors such as Kim Gordon and Patti Smith have published a range of literary titles (photographic collections, poetry, edited volumes) others have continued to write memoirs; Viv Albertine (two to date), Patti Smith (at least three), and Cosey Fanni Tutti (two). Patti Smith is the most published in view of her many volumes of poetry, the creative practice with which she closely identifies. Several have become visual artists, and designers in a variety of media (Chrissie Hynde, Patti Smith, Viv Albertine, Brix Smith Start). Cosey Fanni Tutti has engaged experimental – underground – visual and sonic idioms from the outset, these overlaps a line of continuity in her autobiographical narrative.[245] Others have continued to take public political stances, support 'anti-establishment' lifestyles and mores (Black, Bag, Brownstein, Hynde, and Cosey in particular). Cosey sums up the sense of achievement and wonder in this regard on recalling her graduation with a Master of Arts from the Open University (UK):

'For the previous…years, and in between the many other activities, I had studied hard, written many assignments, sat nerve-racking exams, and now I was being awarded a first-class honours degree. I was stunned and felt like it wasn't really me that had done it all. … I was all dressed up in a graduation gown and mortarboard, with everyone staring at me.'[246]

Alice Bag, who was hoping to study law, went on to win a place on the post-graduate Accelerated Teaching Program at the University of Southern California (USC). She recalls her graduation this way:

'At the end of the summer quarter in 1984, I received my bachelor's degree in philosophy. I didn't attend the ceremony, but my parents were thrilled when I got my certificate in the mail.'[247]

The power of the memoirs as a cumulative, living archive of achievements incorporate the full spectrum of human endeavour, from child-raising to crowd-surfing, from life in the suburbs to mixing in the studio, from advocating social justice causes to going fishing, leaving and (re)forming old and new bands and/as partners, healing or retreating from complicated family relationships, and coming to terms with their own creative arcs and life-paths within an industry that remains unremittingly skewed in favour of androcentric experiences, prowess, and critique.

The vignettes below are by way of drawing this study of ten women – musicians – artists – memoirists to a close. They are brief reflections on selected themes from the memoirs, or moments from beyond the printed page that linger, for this reader at least. They are not signalling an aesthetic or intellectual judgement for my part. There is plenty of informational, journalist and scholarly writing, and fan sites online for exploring any one of these authors now their punk personae have morphed into other domains and interests. The interconnections that the authors have been forging between their own back catalogues, recent work, personal and creative relationships lie between the lines, sometimes as explicit episodes (such as Nina Hagen or Chrissie Hynde meeting Viv Albertine, or Cosey Fanni Tutti encountering the Slits as punk-audience members, Alice Bag seeing Patti Smith perform for the first time, Pauline Black being part of an ad hoc photo shoot with other memoirists before they became published authors), from individual artistic lives and in terms of how the memoir-set can be engaged as a collective public archive of how punk *women* music politics.

Patti Smith Requiems

Another leitmotiv in Smith's memoir writing is the sense of loss. The word requiem is used a lot. But this is also a means through which Smith can cast her life, lived and present-day, in terms of past and ongoing intimate relationships.[248] Some might claim that musically Smith has not done anything as good as her first couple of albums, *Horses* in particular. That said, her repertoire includes hits such as 'Power to the People' written with her late husband Fred (Sonic) Smith, and 'Because the Night'.[249] Smith talks at some length in *Just Kids* about how she prepared for that first live performance in St Mark's Church, considering through this first memoir other significant moments in her own song-writing; for instance on writing 'Work Song' for Janis Joplin, or 'Wild Leaves' the poem in memory of Robert Mapplethorpe that she then put to music.[250]

More recently, Smith has been working with her daughter, Jesse Paris Smith. Together with the band Soundwalk Collective they released a remix, cover album of Nico tracks entitled *Killer Road (A Tribute to Nico)* in 2016, the cover art penned by Patti Smith who also co-wrote the liner notes. Nico (1938-1988, born Christa Päffgen), the female vocalist in the early years of the New York "proto-punk" band Velvet Underground released several solo albums, idiosyncratic and non-conformist tracks for solo voice and harmonium which have gathered increased critical attention through the years.[251] Nico's influence on her generation and subsequent generations of women making music beyond the commercial genre, or industry grooming continues: In 2007 core members of Throbbing Gristle (TG) got together, Cosey recounts this was the last time, at the London Institute of Contemporary Arts (ICA), to record their cover version of Nico's 1970 album, *Desertshore* as a live gig. The TG album of the same name was never released in that format. Rather, as a 'document of the creative process of recording [their] *Desertshore*, we produced a limited-edition twelve-CD wallet set of the entire three days' as Cosey recalls.[252] Smith's collaboration with Soundwalk Collective since the Nico tribute album has produced three albums with her spoken-word and artwork, featuring as well as a major exhibition at the Pompidou Centre in Paris in 2022-23, an event headlining Smith's persona as poet and visual artist even if some coverage focused on her role as 'high priestess of punk'. Smith, in all cases, wears it well.

Pauline Black OBE

The Selecter have reunited yet again with various line-ups, Arthur 'Gaps' Hendrickson and Pauline Black now touring and cutting new records as original members. Black's interregnum career in Black theatre is where her memoir marks the intersection of race, class, and gender that the 2-tone movement brought into the contemporaneous punk scenes focusing on anti-racism and social justice in the UK context. Headed up by three pioneering bands, the Selecter, Madness, and the Specials, Black's role in bringing a race politics sensibility to the multicultural back-catalogue of the punk era calls for more research. The music and its melodies may sound uncomplicated, the dancing joyful, and the ska/reggae beats celebratory, yet the message that multiculturalism is worth fighting for, that black and ethnic minority populations still endure 'too much pressure', remains as urgent as ever. In an interview with Miranda Sawyer promoting the release of their 2023, *Human Algebra*, Black notes that while there was 'much to admire about the 2-Tone movement – the music, the anti-racist, anti-sexist stance, the unity politics – but, of course, it was much easier to be a white man within it than a black woman.'[253]

The album's lyrical subject matter underscores themes from Black's memoir; the sounds, look (Black and Hendrickson in smart black and white, 2-tone, ensembles), and moves familiar albeit with the additional depth of more mature bodies. What is striking in this interview is Black's reference to the well-known photograph taken in 1980, one of her and Poly Styrene posing together with Chrissie Hynde, Debbie Harry, Viv Albertine, and Siouxsie Sioux. Black notes:

'I often look at the picture because I've got it in my toilet. We were all interested in one another, but I see the expressions on my and Poly's faces and they're decidedly different from the others' expressions... We're like: "What are we doing here? Where do we fit into all this?"'[254]

Now entrenched in punk iconographies, the photo takes on other connotations, as it must.

Alice Bag Educator

Alice Bag's second book, *Pipe Bomb for the Soul*, published in 2015, is her diary of her trip to Sandinista-ruled Nicaragua of the 1980s, spending time in a village as a school teacher under the mentoring of local Sandinista community leaders where literacy programs put Nicaragua, along with Cuba, at the top of the educational charts for state-funded programs focused on improving the lives of predominantly poor, illiterate populations. The diary relates Bag's growing awareness that being Hispanic, Latinx from Los Angeles with a bilingual teaching degree was not immediately a way into understanding everyday life in Latin America. The trip follows directly from Bag's teaching experience in schools with mainly English as a Foreign Language pupils such as 'gang-infested Koreatown' in Los Angeles. She recalls her own struggles as a new entrant at school who spoke only Spanish as she finds what she considers her calling helping young children 'acquire English skills with the kindness, patience and understanding that I wish some of my own teachers had shown me'. She has continued to work in education and community projects and releasing solo albums.[255]

Nina Hagen Talking to God

There is a video of Nina Hagen on stage reading aloud from her memoir as well as others in which we see and hear her 'talking to God'. Her delivery, spoken word in this case, centre-stage under a single spotlight is as (melo)dramatic as ever; like having an opera singer reading you a bedtime story. Hagen's memoir is full of biblical quotations as she recounts time spent in India on an ashram, her drug addiction and rediscovery of Christianity. Spirituality are topics that Bag (raised Catholic) and Smith (raised Jehovah's Witness on her mother's side), with Smith Start to a point, broach in their memoirs but Hagen pulls out all the stops as each life-episode is prefaced or exited with a chunk of biblical extracts.

Chrissie Hynde Art and Activism

Musically Hynde has always excelled in punk-inflected pop songs, evident in the 2020 album, *Hate for Sale*, with the Pretenders, with whom Hynde still performs and tours. Her contralto voice lends itself well to jazz and blues vocal lines along with Bob Dylan covers which she released in 2021 as *Standing in the Doorway: Chrissie Hynde Sings Bob Dylan*. Her vocal qualities we can hear on her 2019 solo album with the Valve Bone Woe Ensemble, *Valve Bone Woe*. Not unlike Annie Lennox some years earlier, Hynde concentrates on covers that select from the combined songbook of mainly Anglo-American jazz, blues and musical standards.[256] Hynde has also publicly campaigned on behalf of the imprisoned Wikileaks founder and imprisoned journalist, Julian Assange and animal rights.

Figure 18: Diptych: Chrissie Hynde and Nina Hagen
Artist: Mauricio Escobar (all rights reserved)

Kim Gordon Experiments

Gordon ends her memoir with her experiences of making experimental music with others, careful to distinguish between these ventures and the pressures that marketing would impose on musicians by pigeon-holing them according to musical genres, of which punk is but one. With Sinead Gleeson, Gordon has co-edited a collection of essays by women about women in music, *This Woman's Work*, marking a more explicit awareness of the politics of gender inclusion than she implies in the memoir. As bassist and guitarist Gordon also composes for contemporary dance, releasing solo albums and other collaborative ventures with numerous others. In one video, recorded on a hand-held device, of Gordon performing live a soundtrack she wrote for a modern ballet company she moves, with her guitar in a counter-directional curve , up and down stairwells to the dancers, the drone and feedback loops of her guitar lines working as an improvised call and response to the dancers' movements, replete with *go get 'em* cowboy boots.

Brix Smith Start Extricated

The group the Brix Smith Start has headed up since 2014, Brix & the Extricated, is made up of other former members of the Fall. Mark E. Smith died in 2018 but the Fall itself has had a long list of former, returning, and incoming band members. The Extricated has covered some Fall tracks with Smith Start's vocals more polished, as discussed in Chapter Three. Her time on British television underscores her versatility an embracing of mainstream popular culture; from being a TV Chef to a Fashionista.[257] In 2023 Brix, now billed as Brix Smith, released her first solo album, *Valley of the Dolls* (the 1960s pulp fiction/TV and cinematic reference to Jacqueline Susann's story of young women in show business perhaps lost on some new audiences). Never shy of the mainstream, Brix continues to make music with on her own terms evoking her Californian roots and her time living in Manchester with Mark E. Smith and the Fall.

Carrie Brownstein on TV

Portlandia, a comedy show set in Portland (Oregon) ran on American TV from 2011-2018, starring Carrie Brownstein and Fred Armisen, who both co-wrote the show with Jonathan Krisel. Brownstein reveals in this project her comedy writing and acting skills, the style of the episodes being somewhat improv, home-movie in their tenor. As Brownstein recounts towards the end of her memoir, Sleater-Kinney reunited and began touring again. I managed to get to their Amsterdam show early in 2020, on a Wednesday evening in the Paradiso, and just as the global Covid-19 pandemic was calling a stop to everyday life as we knew it. A different drummer with streamed images and a lowkey lightshow and more backing instrumentals characterized this gig. Brownstein and Corin Tucker remained centre-stage, however. So, when Tucker, in the middle of a track, bent down, fingering the single note on the guitar with one hand as she reached for the water with the other, the shift in stance was striking. Tucker was stepping out of character in the middle of a typically intense Sleater-Kinney track, perhaps revealing the elementary nature of her single-note, single-string technique or her nonchalance about the whole come-back thing.

Cosey After Throbbing Gristle

'It was the first time that working with sound had excited and inspired me. It was exhilarating to explore new ways of creating a different kind of "music"': Cosey Fanni Tutti writes this about the reason she stuck it out with Throbbing Gristle and her relationship with Genesis O-Porridge (Gen), both of which she returns to in both memoirs as she comes to terms with the fundamental dysfunctionality of these two formative – creative and affective – relationships.[258] The second memoir, entitled *Re-Sisters*, is a research based autoethnographic-biographical project that Cosey completed as she worked on the soundtrack for Caroline Catz's 2020 film, *Delia Derbyshire: The Myths & The Legendary Tapes*, on the life and music of Delia Derbyshire. Derbyshire's long under-elucidated or credited legacy for British electronic music was developed during her employment at the BBC Radiophonic Workshop. Her oeuvre includes the theme to the BBC science fiction series *Doctor Who*, for which she has only recently been accredited. In the second memoir Cosey links her lifework with those of Derbyshire (1937-2001)) and mystic Margery Kempe (c. 1373 - c. 1438).[259] Cosey's identification with both these women is unapologetic, to the point of dedicating the book to herself, Derbyshire and Kempe. It is the soundtrack and score that Cosey creates for Catz's documentary on the life of Derbyshire and how she writes about this process as composer and as she collaborates with Catz in the Derbyshire archive that balances out possible accusations of over-identification, if not aggrandisement. I mean, 'why not?!' one could ask.

Viv Albertine Unopened

To Throw Away Unopened is the title of Albertine's second memoir, a requiem (to borrow from Patti Smith) to her father but particularly to her mother whose death, and the aftermath thereof are the emotional core of the book. Albertine discovers a suitcase with the instruction on the lid when sorting out her mother's effects. On opening it (of course she opened it) Albertine discovers mementos her mother saved that provide insights into her father, and her parent's marriage. There is less about (post) punk music scenes, on being a member of the UK's so-called punk royalty, in this book. There is more about sibling rivalry, including a bloodcurdling episode at her mother's deathbed with Viv's estranged younger sister, and coming to terms with an absent, disinterested French-born father while growing up without much money in East London before its rundown working-class neighbourhoods became hipster scenes. In the second memoir Albertine does return to music making as a solo artist, which meant picking up that dreaded guitar again. A passage in the first memoir about a change in the (too close) relationship she had with fellow-Slits member, the much younger Ari Up in the early years is a portent for the themes she considers in her sequel;

'Ari's unhealthy attention comes to an end... It's a bitter-sweet release. At last I'm not under her microscope, but at the same time I'm dismissed. She has more equal relationships now, with people her own age; the same happened to me with my sister. There comes a time when they relish not needing you anymore and move on triumphantly, almost disdainfully. It was painful when my sister did it. I really missed her.'[260]

The candour in passages such as this, where the 'eternal present' merges with things ostensibly in the past, makes your eyes sting.

So, where to now? The punk moniker, in its most working-class and Anglo-American iterations, is, by and large, a white, male and, nominally, anti-establishment signifier; for some, perhaps past its use-by date despite its continual reinventions in its historical heartlands and around the world. In its ideal type of musical form (three 'power chords' based on a major/minor/modal tonality) punk musicality is embedded in the melodic and harmonic progressions underpinning jazz, blues, and mainstream pop music. As Danyel Smith reminds us, these are based on the sounds of Black musicking. In the US high-profile exponents of early-generation punk musicalities and performance codes are less at home in the class-based paradigms of British music criticism and research that predominates in the trade and academic literature. These stereotypes notwithstanding, those women who make a career, as punk/post-punk/riot grrrl/alternative/indie rock acts, are predominantly white. Self-identified Black feminist punk bands such as Big Joanie, founded in the UK in 2013, headline a relatively uncharted area in punkographies and playlists.

Nina Simone – She Who Did It First

If the punk ethic/aesthetic can be, at least partially, boiled down to a performer's lack of deference, even hostility, to their audience then Nina Simone (1933-2003) could well be regarded as a pioneer. Simone's music making is not associated with punk music, nor with punk sartorial style, and certainly not with the sort of anti-capitalist music establishment approach to music performance or recording that is one of punkographies' hallmarks. Simone's work-ethic and approach to making music departs radically from punk DIY ethics and not-for-profit motivations in its ideal form.[261] Simone was a perfectionist, a trained concert pianist, and a gifted musician – a child prodigy – who discovered that she could sing as well as she could play Bach as well as jazz/gospel/blues standards and her own compositions on the piano. Simone's musical legacy and her politics of performance have redefined the blues-jazz-gospel crossroads even though her training, artistic sensibility, and self-awareness of her own talent, were embedded in the – predominantly white and western – classical art music tradition. But it is the way she treated her audience that aligns Simone in certain aspects with first-generations punks' rhetoric against music industry control of performers. Simone had no truck with an audience who could not or would not listen. She was known to leave the stage or refuse to start playing if there was too much noise or restlessness. Her approach was clear from her very first gig, in Atlantic City in the 1950s. Simone recalls:

> 'My attitude to live audiences was formed there at the Midtown, and it's never changed, no matter who the audience or how big the concert hall. If an audience disrespects me it is insulting the music I play and I will not continue, because if they don't want to listen then I don't want to play. ... I don't choose the audience. I don't need them either, and if they don't like my attitude then they don't have to come and see me. Others will.'[262]

Figure 19: Nina Simone (at the piano)
Artist: Mauricio Escobar (all rights reserved)

Revisits to Simone's life as a career musician and the indignities she suffered at the hands of unscrupulous managers, record company executives and intimates, along with testimonies of her being a "difficult woman" with violent tendencies and arguably undiagnosed bipolar disorder, borne out by her daughter, elucidate anecdotes of her no-shows or expressions of exasperation at not being taken seriously by concert promoters or fans:

> 'Some nights my audiences weren't fans but curiosity-seekers who had come to see if I was as difficult as the press said I was – difficult because I objected if people weren't punctual, or didn't take any notice of my instructions for the staging, or didn't

tune my piano properly, or didn't pay me the agreed sum at the contracted time. An audience uninterested in what you have to offer as an artist is the easiest thing in the world to recognize; you feel it the moment you walk out on to the stage.'[263]

Recent scholarship on the intersection of Simone's music-making and her civil rights politics are starting to put this particular record straight: Nina Simone did not separate her music from her politics but neither did she reduce one to the other. She maintained a complex relationship to her own classical training and public stand against racism and discrimination as she made her name as a composer of civil rights anthems and an interpreter of the so-called Great American Songbook. Daphne A. Brooks notes the sonic and performative links between Simone's work and punk's subversion of pop-rock music etiquette in that her influence, ongoing, is through her 'counterintuitive brilliance as an artist who defied the centre, ran circles in the margins, and wove together "highbrow" and "lowbrow" forms to create an off-beat repertoire that was, some might argue, "emo" before "emo." Afropunk, folk eclectic, jazz torch song magic'.[264] These associations are worth more exploration given the overlooked contribution of Black artists to punk as well as experimental avant-garde music making that was happening at the time. Brooks goes on to make the connection between Simone's musico-politics, always rehearsed and staged minutely, to the punk-audience dynamics by noting how 'Simone's fraught relationship with her audience played out in her performances of the songs themselves, and this uniquely tense push and pull with her audiences would prefigure the kinds of (un)ironic modes of haughty aggression and direct critique we often associate with the postmodern glam of a David Bowie, the punk aesthetics of the Sex Pistols, or the hip hop spectacle of a Kanye West.' The staged and, at times, uncontrollable aggression between (ironic) punk poses on stage and punk performance values as a direct critique of mainstream studio pop/rock is encapsulated by the Sid Vicious, and Nina Hagen renditions of 'My Way', a song that Nina Simone made her own some years earlier.[265]

Simone was, in this respect, a vanguard 'she-punk'.[266] In 2023 Simone's would-be 90th birthday was commemorated on mainstream classical and jazz radio stations around the world, her work featuring on BBC Radio 3's playlists that day and in other editions of the station's jazz shows. Her back catalogue featured also on European stations such as Radio Nova (France), NPO Radio 4 (the Netherlands) and so on. Simone in this respect has been granted a place at the table of public music playlists in conventional broadcasting formats. Another reason that makes Simone pertinent to this exploration of how *punk women music politics* is her civil rights activism, her headlining of her sonic art, sartorial decisions and on-stage embodiment (through voice, movement, and speech), her creative practice and politically multiplex consciousness as a racially embedded yet transcendent performativity.[267] Not just for the fact that Simone spent the last years of her life in exile, in Africa, the Caribbean and then in France, becoming prominent in the Martin Luther King movement as well as those of the Malcolm X generations of Black Power politics. She was brought up dirt-poor, during segregation, and came of age during the decade that preceded punk, continuing her career and stardom during the 1970s, and publishing her own memoir, with Stephen Cleary. Her place in this study of women *punking-up* the musicmaking establishment is due, as I note above, to her antithetical attitude to the audience-as-spectator. Simone really did not give a damn. Any video of her live performances shows this disregard for the secular, pop temple-like worship rituals that western popular music made its own and against which Simone also railed.

So I shall lead out with this claim: Nina Simone set the bar for the author-musicians whose memoirs feature in this study; in terms of her willingness to challenge head – on, in the eye, the gender-race-sex stereotypes that remain deeply embedded in the sub-text of how others (music press, academics, fans) might hear or respond to women making music in uncompromising ways; to women generating sound-worlds, embodiments of polymorphous, hyper-sexualized, (non-) heteronormative desirability, and audio-visual production values that push back against essentialisms of the most sexist, racist, classist kind. That Simone's music is of another genus altogether, that as a Black musician and a woman she is considered, *always*, as the exception that proves the rule, underscores the slipperiness of categories when it comes to women and/in the music business.

6. OUTRO

Sex, Gender and Public Culture

> 'What does it feel like to be a woman in a band? I realized that those questions – that talking about the experience – had become part of the experience itself. ... I feel that this meta-discourse...is part of how it feels to be a "woman in music" (or a "woman in anything" for that matter – politics, business, comedy, power). There is the music itself, and then there is the ongoing dialogue about how it feels. The two seem to be intertwined and inescapable. ... I don't know what it's like to be a woman in a band – I have nothing else to compare it to. But I will say that I doubt in the history of rock journalism and writing any man has been asked, "Why are you in an all-male band?"' (Carrie Brownstein)[268]

> 'Boys find it so easy to have girlfriends, there's always a pretty-even smart- girl to be found who's willing to be a sidekick, but it's very difficult for girls to be in the music industry and keep a relationship together. Boys don't like it, not many of them feel comfortable in the supportive role that's required.' (Viv Albertine)[269]

The reflections above, from Brownstein and Albertine who both began in all-women bands, encapsulate the ambivalence they have experienced and encountered as a 'girl in a band'. The double standard by which women are judged, considered effective and legitimated as public figures, is alive and well for creative artists, women in public office and, nowadays, women who have become prominent online, as cultural 'Influencers'. Four decades since punk announced its intention to 'change the record' public culture still pivots on the male experience, opinions, and public imaginaries. There are shifts; more women are writing about and researching music and other arts in public culture, more films and television series are being directed and written by women, featuring powerful characters such as conductors and composers. Radio stations are programming more assiduously female composers from the classical art music world and more music journalists across the spectrum of writing about and reviewing public arts are women.[270] Two themes shape the concluding comments for this exploration of memoirs authored by ten women who made their names during the historical arc of punk rock's timeline; what it means to incorporate listening to (any) music into analytical writing about a musical field or its representatives and, second, some thoughts about punk and its self-proclaimed engagement with current events, local and world politics in other words.

How Did We Get Here?

But first I return to the question of method; some points about how I conducted the study within the research tradition that has shaped the work, introduced in Chapter One and recalled in subsequent chapters through selected key terms and thinkers. The approach is based on a 'lo-fi', that is an analogue cross-referenced 'close reading' of the fifteen books making up the core memoir-set, along with references to other memoirs studied where apposite. What I mean by 'lo-fi' is that I did not deploy digital search tools (except to cross-check page numbers or retrieve passages from digital editions), or 'content analysis' software packages to 'data-scrape' the digitized, manifest content by way of 'coding' methods in order to test a hypothesis or infer generalizable principles about the 'female rock memoir'. Nor did I rely entirely on the other main school of thought in scholarly research into the written word, namely theories of genre, or narratology, which would focus on the book as 'text' and its semantic structure, or draw inferences from the semiotic connotations of the narratives, the authorial 'voice' in the literary sense of the term. I could have deployed any of these methodologies, or a combination thereof. But that would have been a different undertaking.

This does not mean that there is neither a commitment to methodical work nor a lack of theoretical ambition, for this study is written with an academic sensibility. Two approaches governed how I read, re-read, and cross-referenced the 'primary source' material (the published matter) and the analytical conclusions drawn through the curation of the thematic content under discussion. First, I have taken this selection of books from the growing literature of first-hand accounts from women and their life as (punk) musicians as a prism through which to consider academic and journalistic studies of the same period and its subsequent public imaginaries. Second, I treat the memoir-set as a polyvalent collective, a diverse whole in order to take singular, and successive titles seriously as musico-cultural archives, not simply marketing ploys or passing fashion in which female actors get top billing. As argued at the outset, marketing gimmick or not, the rise of the 'femoir' has much to offer scholars of music and politics as an *intersectional* domain. Punk, always a contested notion between its more restricted and more inclusive meanings, has become the object of concerted musicological analysis alongside sociological, popular music research, and political science treatises. The public record and discography of these lifetimes sound and look different as a result. They can be put to work as substantive, primary sonic and visual material for research into first-generation and subsequent iterations of 'punk'.

Some caveats follow: This is not a claim for full coverage or a definitive analysis. None of the memoirs are impervious to alternative interpretations or criticisms from readers or pundits. Nor is the memoir-set I have worked with the only possible 'sample' from this genus of women writing about (making) music. Approaching the texts as primary material does, however, allow them to "speak." to provide that missing sense of 'another voice', to recall Carol Gilligan's work discussed in Chapter Three, to *malestream* monologues about the historical legacy of punk as an expression of political musicmaking. The authors, in their own words, offer an invitation to consider lives and artistic output as complex, not reducible to biologically essentialised judgements about what it takes for women to be present, active and creative under the spotlight of the global cultural industries' entanglement with local, regional and global politics. The challenge has been, and remains, in how to maintain nuance about minority (mis)representation in public domains given the at times cliché-ed positions taken on the sexual politics of 'great works' and 'great artists' in public and academic debates. As Judith Peraino observes, looking to avoid 'widening the gender gap and building rock music [and politics] as a battlefield rather than a discursive field of the sexes' is an occupational hazard for enterprises such as this one claiming a place at the intersection of culture, politics and society.[271] Moreover, as much as these memoirs are testimony to their pioneering role as artists, musicians and writers, the authors are writing from relatively privileged positions. They do so within a sociocultural and commercial domain that remains deeply skewed in gender, race, and class terms for creative expression and opportunity.

Listening to Music Writing

'The shows happened and people liked us. The band [the Pretenders] was magic one night, but inconsistent and shit the rest. I never knew what to expect. But that's what's good about a show – the unpredictability. It's sex after all.' (Chrissie Hynde)[272]

'[W]e just never thought to create a narrative other than the one we were living, ever thought to heighten the story. The music was the only story. It really felt like a scratch or a scrawl – it didn't have an intentional design but you could read into it, you could wonder about it; the mystery was in the plainness, the starkness.' (Carrie Brownstein)[273]

The viscerality of making, listening and dancing to any music is a given in non-Western musical cultures. In the rarefied heights of Western (European and now American) narratives of modernity, in which notions of high art are given pride of place, the connection between sound and body have become severed. Enlightenment thought's privileging of the ('civilised') mind over the ('savage') body and its partnership with Empire and Colonialism, through the enslavement of world majority populations whose music making lies at the epicentre of the Global North's playlists, has indelibly marked Western music production and consumption, writing, and distribution.

Musicologists and music researchers in other disciplines traditionally concentrate on music as a domain, an object of analysis that is based on the 'organization of sound', an influential working definition of music from the composer Edgar Varèse (1883-1965) according to which the formal aspects of any given work (be it a symphony, a blues track, or a Beatles song) can be broken down into its component parts: (sonic) compositions as form according to criteria such as melody, harmony, rhythm, timbre, instrumentation, the production 'mix'. Academic music research proceeds along the main trunk lines of a Western history of music, classical or popular, divided into epochs (such as the Baroque, or Romantic periods), characterised by generic categories (genres) and performed by an A-to-Z of male 'Headliner' personalities (e.g. Bach, Bacharach, Basie, Beatles, Beethoven), While necessary for analytical purposes in delineating a philosophical or empirical line of thought (and many composers and songwriters have reflected on if not written theoretical treatises on their creative practice) the above ethno- and androcentric nomenclature must be considered as a 'temporary thing', recognized for its standardisation and codification impulse rather than its veracity. In practice the divisions are less tidy, their putative progenitors less inclined to be disciplined into reified analytical categories and epochs, often frustrated by other insidious lines of inclusion-exclusion, in terms of public recognition and financial compensation, such as race, class, gender, and religious affiliation.

Social theorists and philosophers in the mid-twentieth century were not unaware of the changes that sound recording technologies, along with the avant-garde's challenges to arts and music establishment were ringing within the classical art music world. Stadium rock music, electronic avant-garde composers, and DIY movements such as punk and early hip-hop were all making 'new' sounds. Recording companies and state agencies have been quick to instrumentalize, when not discriminating against non-conformist sound-worlds. State interventions reached a frenzy during the Culture Wars of the 20th Century Cold War years (namely, American versus Soviet patronage of the arts) and anxious powerbrokers continue to lurk in the background: active in the dynamics of direct censorship and public condemnation as artists not conforming to the industry or national cultural norm become public targets. Roland Barthes represents the awareness, from a western European high-culture perspective to be sure, of such shifts in the very short essay, *Musica Practica*, discussed in Chapter Four. He notes in the opening passage:

> 'There are two musics (at least so I have always thought): the music one listens to, the music one plays. These two musics are totally different arts, each with its own history, its own sociology, its own aesthetics, its own erotic.'[274]

What punk did, within its demographics and historical moment, was bring these two 'totally different arts' into the same 'rough' sonic and embodied frame. Punk's premise was, and is, that the music you listen to, go to hear live can also be music you can play, that anyone can, in principle, play. That is the cultural legacy, I would argue, of *punk*'s challenge to the status quo; other musical forms and practices mount their own challenges. Women who made their way within this founding sensibility show, in their respective recollections, what this merging of the domains of reception and practice that Barthes designates as 'two musics' (at least two) can offer for performer, listener and, now, reader of their memoirs.

Punk and Current Events

It has become a truism of sorts in the third decade of this century to note how polarized society, and public politics have become. Punk emerged, as authors like Black, Bag, and Hynde remind us, in a comparable crucible of sociocultural, economic, and political fury; the 1970s and into the 1980s. Perhaps for every generation it is a time of strong stands, global issues (climate crises to civil wars to police violence to never-ending violence against women). And if so, there are musics that articulate, mobilize, and convey their respective generations' desire for a better world. The memoirists are neither soothsayers nor elected politicians. Their public profiles together with their accounts of personal lives will speak to readers in all sorts of ways even those who may not be familiar with the authors' back-catalogues; judged variously as not 'reckless enough' or 'too self-absorbed' or, worse still, 'too ordinary'. Artists who have been on the public stage for the longest time still have to deal with a barrage of disapproval when taking a public stand on current events, or political controversies. For instance, in the self-identified conservative *National Review*, one columnist paints a scathing portrait of 'aging protesters' in light of Chrissie Hynde and Neil Young's differing, albeit evolving, public stances towards former US President Donald Trump.[275]

Such moments, from the populist American press in this case, underscore ongoing divisions around 'how widely or narrowly one defines political action'[276] With this observation Judith Peraino puts her finger on a sore spot, turf war even, for academic and public debates about the 'proper' relationship between the arts and culture (music in this case) and formal political domains, namely governing institutions and their (state and intergovernmental) representatives. Fully developed contributions to such debates are not spelled out in the memoirs. With the exception of Brownstein and Cosey who step out of their autobiographical narratives to make meta-level commentaries about what, for them, defines or confines political action, the connections are implicit, allusions. Authors make many references to the opportunities that punk, as a historical moment and would-be sociopolitical movement with its anti-commercialism politics of creativity and performance, gave to getting many acts started. Carrie Brownstein recalls, during a tour of Australia with Sleater-Kinney, that 'everyone seemed to have their own version of Riot Grrrl and their interpretation of punk rock feminism; these created a shorthand. It was reassuring to come across what felt like a network of people finding their voices for the first time. Those individual expressions formed a collective force, one that may have been lacking in refinement but was deeply sincere.'[277] In the case of Patti Smith, the post-Beat Generation and Greenwich Village/Chelsea Hotel scenes in New York of the 1960s and 1970s provides the backdrop to her recollections in *Just Kids*. Smith and Chrissie Hynde, and to a certain extent Brix Smith Start and Viv Albertine, it is the cultural and political upheavals of the Vietnam War and rise of explicitly political folk and rock music that mark their youth: Hynde recollects being on the campus during the 1970 shootings of four Kent State University students in Ohio, USA, during an anti-Vietnam war protest; for Alice Bag, Carrie Brownstein, and Kim Gordon punk music mixing with experiments in the rock music sound palette (where Sonic Youth, and Sleater-Kinney made their mark) were part of the 1980s-90s. Conventional understandings of (world) politics are echoed in their responses to the policies of respective US administrations. Nina Hagen's life is embedded in the Cold War divides and the fall of the Berlin Wall, with Nina Simone engaging publicly on stage, and on the streets, for civil rights in the US and around the world. For the UK based authors (Albertine, Black, Smart, Hynde, and Cosey) political mobilization at home was about Thatcherism (the austerity policies of Margaret Thatcher's Conservative governments) and the rise of the xenophobic, racist nationalist right in British politics.

Successive Gulf Wars in Iraq and the September 11 attacks in 2001 on the World Trade Centre in New York are world current events that have touched the lives of nearly all the memoirists. For instance, writing about the geopolitical context in which the 2002 Sleater-Kinney album, *One Beat*, was released and her ambivalence about its positioning as an explicitly political album, Brownstein notes how 'writing songs after 9/11 felt treacherous' in the face of 'the xenophobia and jingoism that took hold of the culture post-9/11'. She articulates a challenge for explorations into the crossovers between musical, cultural and political concerns: in the case of this album 'big power' politics, national crisis, are contained in the same playing time as the vernacular of everyday emotional experience (see Chapter Three). As Brownstein observes, the conventional, formal 'political landscape was not the only thing fuelling our song writing or the element that defined the sound on our next record' after *One Beat*.[278]

Figure 20: Kim Gordon
Artist: Mauricio Escobar (all rights reserved)

The tension between different levels of analysis – politics as mundane or grandstanding – are thrown into relief at times of crisis, national and global, or when public institutions or public figures make overtly politicised gestures from funding to running for public office. Yet there are political and cultural movements for change that consider the arts as integral, not simply an afterthought, the soundtrack for more significant performances; election campaigns and rallies, fund-raising events, or award ceremonies. A spokesperson for Diem25 (the abbreviation for *Democracy in Europe Movement 2025*), a 'pan-European, progressive movement' founded in 2016 sums up an understanding of the fundamental interplay thus:

> 'Art is a revolution in itself...doing something just for the sake of creation... for free... And this idea of freedom and creation is revolutionary in as much as it entails consequences concerning power, the power of creation and the alienation of this power... The real revolutionary contribution of art is in pointing out the possibilities of humanity, and creation, and the freedom that is inside these possibilities ...'[279]

For commentators from within the political and cultural establishments of the Anglo-American hegemonic axis, the policy dimensions at stake are those around equity, representation, and entitlement. Music and art critics engage in these conversations as well: As Lucy Caplan argues, in a review of how African American music is being curated and exhibited in public museums in the US, 'music – and especially African American music, which is the lifeblood of American music – is inescapably intertwined with politics.'[280] Caplan goes on to argue that positing art and politics as either mutually exclusive, or indistinguishable from one another is missing a deeper issue, namely that:

> 'this connection between music and politics is real and necessary, and the most notable distinction between {these two extremes} is that they point the arrow linking art and politics in opposite directions. ...[to] use music to inspire political action, ... [or to imagine] politics that create a space for art. Either way, making art remains the essential part of the equation.'[281]

Considering the memoirists and their work, along punk 's DIY and marketed timeline, on its primarily Anglo-American geocultural axis, as interlocutors in recurring conversations about art and politics is not immediately apparent. The register in which such memoirs are written, substantive topics discussed, let alone the political affiliations with which any of these authors may identify are not written for academic debates. By virtue of being first-hand accounts, an author's own claims for their work as political or, conversely, not political, unsettles scholarly conventions nonetheless; around what counts as empirical evidence or conceptual rigour. Even as primary sources the accounts defy typecasting, disrupt ideological agendas that would deploy the musical material, or artist for any particular political platform, a recurring theme for authors like Cosey Fanni Tutti or Brownstein in their unease about the 'feminist' label. They do not resonate immediately with those musicians and artists who have made their music a political party vehicle, such as Billy Bragg whose unequivocal British left-wing trade unionist affiliations remain a constant in his music and public appearances, as does the social justice politics of Joan Baez in the US folk music scene, or the political stance that Fela Kuti, founder of Afrobeat, took against the military dictatorship in 1970s Nigeria.

Updating the usual references to music and politics through the lens of the anti-war protest song, the back-catalogue dating for the most part from the mid-twentieth century, how working musicians respond to immediate events became stark during the US Presidency of Donald Trump (2016-2020). The political and cultural aftermath of Trump's time in the White House is still unfurling. At the time artists were prominent mobilizing online, on the streets, and in award ceremonies to express their objections to the Trump administration's policy agendas, sexist and xenophobic pronouncements. Global protests under the *Women's March* banner along with the *Me Too* and *Black Lives Matter* mobilizations include musicians and other artists, in a time-honoured tradition of creative communities pinning their political colours to the mast. Comparable alliances have been taking place since Trump's defeat in the 2020 Presidential election in the UK and European Union countries in the face of rising xenophobia, and right-wing extremist electoral campaigns. Yet as Carrie Brownstein herself notes, the pressure to make overtly political music has creative and aesthetic implications for how an artist perceives and experiences her own work:

> 'We had spent years attempting to exist free of excess and arbitrary labels that were not descriptions of our music: female, indie, queer. Riot Grrrl, post-Riot Grrrl music. Now here we were with the potentiality of being a "political" band. But in the interim years we'd realized that denial is a form of compliance and self-erasure. Plus, it's exhausting. We would go out on the road and play these songs and people could interpret them however the hell they wanted.'[282]

Brownstein's qualms are about more than being precious about labels, or her still smarting from fallouts with former creative intimates, or the misappropriation or misrepresentation of one's creative output. Brownstein is reflecting on the implications for how an artist may choose to render her political interests or responses to current events: as manifest content (angry lyric), or in more metaphorical, impressionistic terms through poetic devices, analogies or the sonic mix; a characteristic of how Smith Start discusses the way personal and current events were combined elements in her song writing with Mark E. Smith (see Chapter Three).

The tension between 'denial and compliance' for artists in the face of any public political or cultural crisis, the Russian invasion of Ukraine in 2022 as one pressing example on going to press let alone the ongoing Civil War in Syria, speaks to controversies in academe and music and arts journalism about how to change the way we think, and write about the arts-politics nexus: how to do so, in ways that do justice to the art form without eliding its historical context or its demographic complexities.[283] As a wave of studies on women and music across the spectrum, 'lost' composers and bands, from periods like punk, builds, it is worth taking a leaf out of G. Douglas Barrett's book, *After Sound*. In this polemic against the constraints of disciplinary research paradigms he looks to 'reimagine music as a critically engaged art form in dialogue with contemporary art, continental philosophy, and global politics'. Barrett rejects both the legacy of treating music as a thing-in-itself, for the 'absolute music' tradition continues to predominate classical, western music research, and 'sound art' or sound studies, perceived as some polar opposite. Barrett advocates stretching the very category of music – and implicitly that of politics I would argue, by suspending 'the notion of music as a series of discrete sounds identifiable as tones, or "notes" with determinate pitches etc. and which, taken together, compose what is commonly referred to as a musical work'. He wants to show that there are artists and performers who have been challenging the notion that music and/as sound are immutably linked by returning to a pre-modern notion of music as '*not* sound art' in the first place.[284]

Figure 21: Nina Simone
Artist: Mauricio Escobar (all rights reserved)

I still would not want to go quite as far in stipulating that 'music', as an object of analysis and medium for sociocultural and political agency, should be completely stripped of the sonic. That said, the memoirs explored here do go some way in affirming projects that consider music as 'not an object but a process engaging bodies, time, and space.'[285]

Fade Up

'I felt, watching Jim Morrison, that I could do that. I can't say why I thought this. I had nothing in my experience to make me think that would ever be possible, yet I harbored that conceit. ... I had no stage fright and liked to elicit a response from the audience.' (Patti Smith)[286]

The 15 memoirs explored here are written by women who, by virtue of their age and the place they have in their respective musical generations, are proudly 'old guard'. As individual, personal accounts that double up as public socio-musicological archives, these books provide signposts for scholars interested in exploring the music-politics-culture nexus as a multisited, audiovisual, and multidimensional constellation. I turn again to Simone de Beauvoir as she brings to a close *All Said and Done*, the final volume of her own memoir-set: 'This time I shall not write a conclusion ... I leave the reader to draw any [they] may choose.'[287] This challenge – to think independently – from Beauvoir, 'another girl, another planet',[288] resonates with fundamental aspect of punk's cultural and political legacy; works of sight and sound to which women, from across the vicissitudes of class, race, gender, sexuality and worldviews continue to make their mark.

APPENDIX: THE MEMOIR-SET

Viv Albertine (b. 1954)
Clothes, Clothes, Clothes. Music, Music, Music. Boys, Boys, Boys: A Memoir (2014)
To Throw Away Unopened: A Memoir (2018)

Alice Bag (b. 1958)
Violence Girl: East L.A. Rage to Hollywood Stage, a Chicana Punk Story (2011)
Pipe Bomb for the Soul (2015)

Pauline Black (b. 1953)
Black by Design: A 2-Tone Memoir (2011)

Carrie Brownstein (b. 1974)
Hunger Makes Me a Modern Girl: A Memoir (2015)

Kim Gordon (b. 1953)
Girl in a Band: A Memoir (2015)

Nina Hagen (b. 1955)
Bekenntnisse (Confessions) (2011)

Chrissie Hynde (b. 1951)
Reckless: My Life as a Pretender (2016)

Patti Smith (b. 1946)
Just Kids (2010)
M Train (2015)
Year of the Monkey (2017)

Brix Smith Start (b. 1962)
The Rise, The Fall, and The Rise (2016)

Cosey Fanni Tutti (b. 1951)
Art, Sex, Music (2017)
Re-Sisters (2022)

BIBLIOGRAPHY

Albertine, Viv, 2014. *Clothes, Clothes, Clothes. Music, Music, Music. Boys, Boys, Boys: A Memoir,* Thomas Dunn.
Albertine, Viv. 2018. *To Throw Away Unopened: A Memoir.* London: Faber and Faber.
Bag, Alice. 2011. *Violence Girl: East L.A. Rage to Hollywood Stage, a Chicana Punk Story.* Port Townsend WA: Feral House.
Bag, Alice. 2015. *Pipe Bomb for the Soul.* Los Angeles: Alice Bag Publishing.
Badgley, William E. (Dir.). 2017. *Here to be Heard: The Story of the Slits.* Documentary. Head Gear Films. 1 hr. 26 mins.
Barkin, Elaine, and Lydia Hamessley, eds. 1999. *Audible Traces: Gender, Identity, and Music.* Zürich; Los Angeles: Carciofoli.
Barrett, G. Douglas, 2016, *After Sound: Toward a Critical Music,* London: Bloomsbury.
Barthes, Roland. 1977. *Image – Music – Text.* Trans. Stephen Heath. New York: Hill and Wang.
Bayton, Mavis. 1998. *Frock Rock: Women Performing Popular Music.* London: Oxford University Press.
Beaumont-Thomas, Ben. 2022. "Pamela Rooke, punk rock fashion icon known as Jordan, dies aged 66." *The Guardian.* 4 April 2022; https://www.theguardian.com/music/2022/apr/04/pamela-rooke-punk-rock-fashion-icon-jordan-dies-aged-66.
de Beauvoir, Simone. (1949) 1972. *The Second Sex.* Trans. H M Parshley. Penguin.
de Beauvoir, Simone, (1960) 1962, *The Prime of Life,* Vol. 2, Penguin Books.
de Beauvoir, Simone, (1972) 1977, *All Said and Done,* Vol.5, Penguin Books.
Bell, Celeste and Howe, Zoe. 2019. *Dayglo!: The Poly Styrene Story.* Omnibus Press.
Birch, Gina and Reddington, Helen. 2018. *Stories from the She-Punks.* Documentary.
Black, Pauline. 2011. *Black by Design: A 2-Tone Memoir.* London: Serpent's Tail.
Bleiker, Roland. 2009. *Aesthetics and World Politics.* London: Palgrave Macmillan.
Bowers, Jane and Tick, Judith (eds), 1987, *Women Making Music: The Western Art Tradition, 1150-1950,* University of Illinois Press.
Bowers, Jane M. 1989. Feminist Scholarship and the Field of Musicology: I College Musiic Symposium Vol. 29 (1989), pp. 81-92 College Music Society.

Bowers, Jane, 2002, Current Issues in Feminist Musical Scholarship: Representation and Gender Performance, Identity and Subjectivity, and Telling Stories about Women's Musical Lives, IAWM Journal (2002); http://iawm.org/stef/articles_html/bowers_women_musicology.html.

Broad, Leah. 2023. *Quartet: How Four Women Changed the Musical World*. London: Faber.

Brooks, Daphne A. 2011. Nina Simone's Triple Play, in *Callaloo*. Vol. 34, No. 1 (Winter, 2011), pp. 176-197.

Brownstein, Carrie, 2015, *Hunger Makes Me a Modern Girl: A Memoir*. New York: Riverhead Books.

Butler, Judith. 2006 [1990]. *Gender Trouble: Feminism and the Subversion of Identity*. Routledge.

Caplan, Lucy, 2017, 'Variations: Lucy Caplan on Music in Moments of Crisis – The Log Journal'. 2017. http://thelogjournal.com/2016/11/23/variations-lucy-caplan-on-music-in-moments-of-crisis/. Accessed February 9.

Coen, Joe. 2012. "Punk Feminism: Up the Pinks!" *Huck*, August 1. https://www.huckmag.com/perspectives/reportage-2/punk-feminism/.

Collins, Patricia Hill and Bilge, Sirma. 2020. *Intersectionality*, 2nd Edition. Cambridge UK: Polity.

Connell, R. W. and Messerschmidt, James W. 2005. Hegemonic Masculinity: Rethinking the Concept. *Gender and Society*. Volume 19, Issue; https://doi.org/10.1177/0891243205278639.

Coon, Caroline, "Punk Rock: Rebels Against the System." *Melody Maker*, 7 August 1976; https://www.rocksbackpages.com/Library/Article/punk-rock-rebels-against-the-system.

Crenshaw, Kimberlé. 2003, "Traffic at the Crossroads; Multiple Oppressions" in *Sisterhood Is Forever: The Women's Anthology for a New Millennium*, edited by Robin Morgan. New York: Washington Square Press: 43-57.

Davies, M. (2005). Do It Yourself Punk Rock and the Disalienation of International Relations. In: *Resounding International Relations: On Music, Culture, and Politics*. (ed) M.I. Franklin. New York: Palgrave Macmillan: 113-140. https://doi.org/10.1007/978-1-137-05617-7_6.

Davies, M. and Franklin, M.I. 2015. What does (the Study of) World Politics Sound Like? In: F. Caso and C. Hamilton, eds., *Popular Culture and World Politics: Theories, Methods, Pedagogies*. Bristol, UK: E-International Relations Publishing, pp. 120-147.

Diamond, Beverley, 2002, Elaine Barkin and Lydia Hamessley, eds. 1999. Audible Traces: Gender, Identity, and Music, Tullia Magrini, ed. 2003. Music and Gender: Perspectives from the Mediterranean. Review in Canadian University Music Review, vol. 24, n° 1, 2003: 118-125.

Diem25. 2021. *E41: How can art be used to create political change?* 22 July 2021; https://www.youtube.com/watch?v=Y9XOGF-xM_M (accessed 10 April 2023).

Downes, Julia. 2007. Riot Grrrl: The legacy and contemporary landscape of feminist cultural activism. Academia.edu; https://www.semanticscholar.org/paper/Riot-Grrrl%3A-The-legacy-and-contemporary-landscape-Downes/027ac319bbc3623407fe1c75fdca66d0c164468f.

Downes. Julia. 2012. The Expansion of Punk Rock: Riot Grrrl Challenges to Gender Power Relations in British Indie Music Subcultures. Academia.edu; https://www.academia.edu/20964857/The_Expansion_of_Punk_Rock_Riot_Grrrl_Challenges_to_Gender_Power_Relations_in_British_Indie_Music_Subcultures?auto=download&email_work_card=download-paper =.

Dunn, Kevin, 2016 *Global Punk: Resistance and Rebellion in Everyday Life*. London: Bloomsbury. https://doi.org/10.5040/9781501314636.ch-001.

Dunn, Kevin, 2005, The Clash of Civilization: Notes from a Punk Scholar, in *Resounding International Relations: On Music, Culture, and Politics*, (ed) M.I. Franklin, New York: Palgrave Macmillan: 263-284.

Edgers, Geoff, 2015. 'Rise of the Female Rock Memoir'. *The Washington Post*, September 4. https://www.washingtonpost.com/entertainment/music/rise-of-the-female-rock-memoir/2015/09/04/64db029e-5097-11e5-933e-7d06c647a395_story.html?utm_term=.1734af2d4b12 accessed 2 February 2017.

Evans, Liz (ed), 1997, *Women Performing Popular Music: Girls Will Be Boys: Women Report on Rock*, Pandora Press.

Feldman, Zeena and Hakim, Jamie. 2020. From Paris is Burning to #dragrace: Social media and the celebrification of drag culture. *Celebrity Studies*, 11 (4). pp. 386-401.

Feldstein, R. (2005). 'I don't trust you anymore': Nina Simone, Culture, and Black Activism in the 1960s. *Journal of American History*, vol. 91(4), pp. 1349-1379. https://doi.org/10.2307/3660176.

Fontana, Kaitlin, 2012, The Rise of the Femoir, Hazlitt, 23 August, 2012: http://hazlitt.net/longreads/rise-femoir.

Franklin, M.I. 2005. *Resounding International Relations: On Music, Culture, and Politics*. New York: Palgrave.

Franklin, M. I. 2020, "Music Making Politics – Beyond Lyrics." in *Politik* Nummer 1 | Årgang 23 | 2020. University of Copenhagen: 51-69.

Franklin, M.I. 2021a. Music: Women Rewriting Punk Performance Politics, in the *Oxford University Press Handbook of Politics and Performance*, (eds) S. Rai, S. Jestrovic, M. Gluhovic, and M. Saward. London/New York: Oxford University Press: 485-499.

Franklin M.I. 2021b, *Sampling Politics: Music and the Geocultural*. New York/London: Oxford University Press.

Freeman, Hadley, 2016, 'The Girl With the Lower Back Tattoo by Amy Schumer Review – the Problem with "femoirs." The Guardian' https://www.theguardian.com/books/2016/sep/09/the-girl-with-the-lower-back-tattoo-review-amy-schumer-autobiography-memoir-femoir Accessed January 25 2017.

Frith, Simon, and Angela McRobbie. [1978] 1990. Rock and Sexuality. *On Record: Rock, Pop and the Written Word*, Simon Frith and Andrew Goodwin (eds). London: Routledge.: 317–32.

Frith, Simon. 2007. *Taking Popular Music Seriously: Selected Essays*. Hampshire UK: Ashgate.

Gaines, M. (2013). The Quadruple-Consciousness of Nina Simone. *Women & Performance: a journal of feminist theory*, vol. (23)2, pp. 248-267. https://doi.org/10.1080/0740770x.2013.825428.

Gardner, Abigail. 2020. *Aging and Contemporary Female Musicians*. London/New York: Routledge.

Gijssel, Robert van. 2017. "New New Wave." *De Volkskrant*, 8 May 2017: V4-5.

Gilligan, Carol. 1983. *In a Different Voice: Psychological Development and Women's Development*. Cambridge Massachusetts/London: Harvard University Press.

Goddard, Michael and Halligan, Benjamin (eds), 2010, *Mark E. Smith and The Fall: Art, Music and Politics*, Ashgate.

Goldman, Vivien. 2019. *Revenge of the She-Punks: A Feminist Music History from Poly Styrene to Pussy Riot*. University of Texas Press.

Gordon, Kim 2014, *Is It My Body? Collected Texts*, edited by Branden W. Joseph, Sternberg Press.

Gordon, Kim. 2015. *Girl in a Band: A Memoir*. New York: Dey Street Books.

Gracyk, Theodore. N.d. "The Aesthetics of Popular Music." Internet Encyclopedia of Philosophy; https://iep.utm.edu/music-po/#H3.

Hagen, Nina. 2010. *Bekenntnisse*. Pattloch.

Harris, John. 2010. *Hail! Hail! Rock "n" Roll: The Ultimate Guide to the Music, the Myths and the Madness*. London: Hachette, Digital/Little, Brown Book Group.

Harry, Debbie (with Sylvie Simmons). 2019. *Face It: A Memoir*. Day St Books.

Haynes, Todd (Dir.). 1998. *Velvet Goldmine*. Feature film written by James Lyons and Todd Haynes.

Hesmondhalgh, David, 2013, *Why Music Matters*, UK: Wiley-Blackwell.

Hess, Liam. 2022. In Memory: Pamela Rooke: The "Queen Of Punk" Known As Jordan, Dies At 66. *Vogue* (UK), 5 April 2022; https://www.vogue.co.uk/arts-and-lifestyle/article/pamela-rooke-jordan-has-died.

Howe, Zoe Street. 2009. *Typical Girls? The Story of The Slits*. London: Omnibus Press.

Hynde, Chrissie. 2016. *Reckless: My Life as a Pretender*. New York: Doubleday.

John, Elton. 2019. *Me*. New York. St Martin's Griffin.

Knausgaard, Karl Ove. 2009. *My Struggle: Book 1*. New York: Farrar, Strauss and Giroux.

Koskoff, Ellen, 2000, Foreword, in *Music and Gender* edited by Moisala, Pirkko, and Beverley Diamond. University of Illinois Press: ix-xiii.

Magrini, Tuilia (ed), 2003, *Music and Gender: Perspectives from the Mediterranean*, University of Chicago Press.

Malott, Curry, and Milagros Peña. 2004. *Punk Rockers' Revolution: A Pedagogy of Race, Class, and Gender*. Oxford: Peter Lang.

Marcus, Greil, 1989, *Lipstick Traces: A Secret History of the Twentieth Century*, Harvard University Press.

Marcus, Sara. 2010. *Girls to the Front: The True Story of the Riot Grrrl Revolution*. New York: Harper Perennial.

Leslie McCall, 2005. The Complexity of Intersectionality. *Signs: Journal of Women in Culture and Society*. Volume 30, Number 3: https://www.journals.uchicago.edu/doi/10.1086/426800.

McClary, Susan. 1991. *Feminine Endings: Music, Gender and Sexuality*. Minnesota: University of Minnesota Press.

McClary, Susan. 1992. *Georges Bizet: Carmen*. Cambridge: Cambridge University Press.

McDonald, Soraya Nadia. 2015. 'Pretenders Frontwoman Chrissie Hynde Says Women Can Be at Fault If They Are Raped'. *The Washington Post*, August 30. https://www.washingtonpost.com/news/arts-and-entertainment/wp/2015/08/30/pretenders-frontwoman-chrissie-hynde-says-women-can-be-at-fault-if-they-are-raped/?utm_term=.11b5e6421252 , accessed 1 February 2017.

McDonnell, Evelyn (ed), 1997, *Rock She Wrote: Women Write about Rock, Pop, and Rap*, Cooper Square Publishers.

McKay, George and Arnold, Gina, 2020 *The Oxford Handbook of Punk Rock*. Oxford University Press; 10.1093/oxfordhb/9780190859565.001.0001.

McKeon, Belinda. 2015. Me, Myself and I in an Age of Autobiographical Fiction. *The Guardian*, August 20. https://www.theguardian.com/books/2015/aug/20/me-myself-i-in-an-age-of-autobiographical-fiction.

Moisala, Pirkko, and Beverley Diamond (eds). 2000, *Music and Gender*. University of Illinois Press.

Molleson, Kate. 2022. *Sound Within Sound: Opening our Ears to the 20th Century*. London: Faber.

Morley, Paul, 2008, *Joy Division: Piece by Piece: Writing about Joy Division 1977-2007*. London: Plexus Publishing.

Noland, Carrie. 1995. Rimbaud and Patti Smith: Style as Social Deviance – 1995, Critical Inquiry. Academia.edu; https://www.academia.edu/18261819/Rimbaud_and_Patti_Smith_Style_as_Social_Deviance?auto=download&email_work_card=download-paper.

O'Sullivan, Sibbie. 2015. '"Reckless" Review: Chrissie Hynde's Memoir Is Part Bravado, Part Regret'. *The Washington Post*, September 1. https://www.washingtonpost.com/entertainment/books/reckless-review-chrissie-hyndes-memoir-is-part-bravado-part-regret/2015/09/01/aadeea80-50f1-11e5-933e-7d06c647a395_story.html?utm_term=.27dc775a8148 accessed 1 February, 2017.

Pearson, David, 2021. *Rebel Music in the Triumphant Empire: Punk Rock in the 1990s United States*. New York: Oxford University Press.

Pelly, Jean. 2019. Kathleen Hanna on What Bikini Kill Means Now. *Pitchfork*. November 22, 2019; https://pitchfork.com/features/interview/kathleen-hanna-interview-what-bikini-kill-means-now/.

Penman, Ian, 2022. Why Solange Matters by Stephanie Phillips. *London Review of Books*. Vol. 44, No. 1. 6 January 2022: 7-9.

Peraino, Judith A. 2001. Review of *Madonna: Bawdy and Soul; Scars of Sweet Paradise: The Life and Times of Janis Joplin; Frock Rock: Women Performing Popular Music, ; Girls Will Be Boys: Women Report on Rock*, by Karlene Faith, Alice Echols, Mavis Bayton, and Liz Evans. *Journal of the American Musicological Society* 54 (3): 692–709.

Peraino, Judith A., 2006, *Listening to the Sirens: Musical Technologies of Queer Identity from Homer to Hedwig*, University of California Press.

Peraino, Judith, Suzanne G. Cusick, Mitchell Morris, Lloyd Whitesell, William Cheng, Maureen Mahon, Sindhumathi Revuluri, Nadine Hubbs, and Stephan Pennington. 2013. 'Music and Sexuality'. *Journal of the American Musicological Society* 66 (3): 825–72.

Petrusich, Amanda. 2019. The Survival of Iggy Pop. *The New Yorker*. August 26, 2019; https://www.newyorker.com/magazine/2019/09/02/the-survival-of-iggy-pop.

Pitchfork. 2016. *The Story of Feminist Punk n 33 Songs*. Introduction by Vivien Goldman. August 8 2016; https://pitchfork.com/features/lists-and-guides/9923-the-story-of-feminist-punk-in-33-songs/.

Raha, Maria and Gordon, Kim, 2004, *Cinderella's Big Score: Women of the Punk and Indie Underground*, Seal Press.

Rai, S. and Reinelt, J. (2014). *The Grammar of Politics and Performance*. London, New York: Routledge. https://doi.org/10.4324/9781315879871.

Rai, S. Jestrovic, M. Gluhovic, and M. Saward (Eds). 2020. *Oxford Handbook of Politics and Performance*. London/New York: Oxford University Press.

Reddington, Helen, 2012. *The Lost Women of Rock Music: Female Musicians of the Punk Era*. Second edition. Sheffield UK: Equinox Publishing.

Reinelt, Janelle and Shirin M Rai, 'Introduction' in Rai, S. and Reinelt, J. (Eds) (2014). *The Grammar of Politics and Performance*, London/New York: Routledge.

Reynolds, Simon. 2022. "Review of The Life and Times of Malcolm McLaren: The Biography by Paul Gorman." *London Review of Books*. Vol. 44 No. 5 · 10 March 2022: 19-24.

Richards, Keith. 2010. *Life*. London/New York: Little, Brown and Company

Rogers, Jude. 2022. *The Sound of Being Human: How Music Shapes Our Lives*. London: White Rabbit.

Ross, Alex. 2010. *The Rest Is Noise: Listening to the Twentieth Century*. New York: Picador.

Ross, Alex. 2011. *Listen to This*. London: Fourth Estate.

Saefullah, Hikmawan, 2017. 'Nevermind the jahiliyyah, here's the hijrahs': Punk and the religious turn in the contemporary Indonesian underground scene. *Punk & Post-Punk*, Volume 6, Number 2, June 2017, pp. 263-289.

Savage, Jon. 1991. *England's Dreaming: Anarchy, Sex Pistols, Punk Rock and Beyond*. New York: St Martin's Griffin.

Sawyer, Miranda. 2023. Interview: The Selecter's Pauline Black: 'When we get on stage, something alchemical happens'. *Guardian*. 9 April 2023; https://www.theguardian.com/music/2023/apr/09/the-selecter-pauline-black-ska-2-tone-human-algebra-interview.

Shaprio, Michael J. 2004. *Methods and Nations: Cultural Governance and the Indigenous Subject*, London and New York: Routledge.

Shaw, Philip. 2008. *Horses*. London/New York: Bloomsbury Academic.

Sheffield, Rob, 2020, The 25 Greatest Rock Memoirs of All Time, in *Rolling Stone Magazine*, 19 December 2020; https://www.rollingstone.com/music/music-lists/books-greatest-rock-memoirs-of-all-time-161198/nikki-sixx-the-heroin-diaries-2007-228907; accessed 18 March 2022.

Shumer, Amy. 2017. *The Girl with the Lower Back Tattoo*. Gallery Books.

Simone, Nina. 2003 (1992). *I Put a Spell on You: The Autobiography of Nina Simone*, with Stephen Cleary, 2nd edition Cambridge, MA: Da Capo Press.

Small, Christopher. 1998. *Musicking: The Meanings of Performing and Listening*. Middletown, CT: Wesleyan University Press.

Smith, Danyel. 2022. *Shine Bright: A Very Personal History of Black Women in Pop*. New York: Roc Lit.

Smith, Patti. 2010. *Just Kids*. London: Bloomsbury.

Smith, Patti. 2015. *M Train*. New York: Knopf.

Smith, Patti. 2017. *Year of the Monkey*.

Smith, Patti with Soundwalk Collective, 2022. *Evidence*, Audio and Video Installation, Centre Pompidou, Paris. 20 October 2022 – 6 March 2023.

Snapes, Laura. 2015. Dissonant Joy: A Guide to Europe's Punk Foremothers. *Pitchfork*, October 2, 2015; https://pitchfork.com/features/pitchfork-essentials/9729-dissonant-joy-a-guide-to-europes-punk-foremothers/.

Start, Brix Smith. 2016. *The Rise, The Fall, and The Rise*. Faber & Faber.

Street, John. 2012. *Music and Politics*. Cambridge, UK: Polity Press.

Thunberg, Greta, Thunberg, Svante, Ernman, Malena, and Emman, Beata. 2020. *Our House Is on Fire: Scenes of a Family and a Planet in Crisis*. Penguin Books.

Tierney, Paul. 2019. "Interview: Jordan, the face of punk: 'The things I wore made people apoplectic', the *Guardian*. 23 April 2019; https://www.theguardian.com/music/2019/apr/23/punk-jordan-mooney.

Tongson, Karen, 2021. *Why Karen Carpenter Matters*. London: Faber.

Tutti, Cosey Fanni. 2017. *Art, Sex, Music*. London: Faber & Faber.

Tutti, Cosey Fanni, 2022. *Re-Sisters: The Lives and Recordings of Delia Derbyshire, Margery Kempe & Cosey Fanni Tutti*. London: Faber.

UN Women. 2022. *Facts and figures: Ending violence against women*. February 2022; https://www.unwomen.org/en/what-we-do/ending-violence-against-women/facts-and-figures.

White, Armond. 2020. Neil Young and Chrissie Hynde: Rock of the Aged Protesters, *National Review*. Feb 27, 2020; https://www.nationalreview.com/2020/02/neil-young-and-chrissie-hynde-rock-of-the-aged-protesters/.

World Health Organization (WHO). 2021. *Violence Against Women: Key Facts*. 9 March 2021; https://www.who.int/news-room/fact-sheets/detail/violence-against-women.

Zalewski, Marysia, 2014, Feminist International Relations: Making Sense, in *Gender Matters in Global Politics: A Feminist Introduction to International Relations*, Laura J. Shepherd (ed). Second Edition. London: Routledge: 3-13.

NOTES

Intro

1. Reddington (2012: 1) and Vivian Goldman (2019). See also Kevin Dunn (2016), Matt Davies (2005), and Pearson (2021) all of whom position themselves as punk practitioners, fans, DJs, and scholars.
2. The books are listed in the appendix as a quick-reference guide.
3. This term was coined by Christopher Small (1998), whose contribution to studies of music as creative communities of practice, rather than form and repertoire, shifted mainstream music in a major way; see Franklin (2005, 2021b).
4. Zalewski, (2014: 7, 9).
5. See Peraino (2001) with respect to the approach taken by Susan McClary in her study of Bizet's opera, *Carmen* (1992) and the range of perspectives from contributors in the *Music and Sexuality* Colloquy (Peraino and Cusick, 2013).
6. McRobbie (in Gardner 2020).
7. See Davies and Franklin (2015), Goldman (2019: 78-81), and Barrett (2016: 63 passim) for thoughts on Pussy Riot's political and cultural influence within a punk sensibility. See Dunn (2016) and Saefullah (2017) for more on punk articulations in a global context, including punk scenes in Muslim-majority countries such as Indonesia.
8. Gzowksi (1977), Coon (1976).
9. Reddington (2012: 1, 6, 7, 128, 131). Dunn (2016) and Pearson (2021) provide other (anti-) definitional nuances.
10. This archived clip became part of Iggy Pop's Twitter feed decades later, tweeted with reference to Pop's first BBC Radio 6 radio show in which Pop notes that his diatribe from 1977 is sampled in the Mogwai track "Punk Rock" (1999). Iggy Pop continues in this vein, two decades after the Mogwai homages, as he recalls his moment on TV by noting, "yeah, I still recall the conversation and what a drag it was being on hosted TV coz all those TV hosts really suck..." (Iggy Pop 2021 cited from @BBC6Music, Twitter, October 13, 2021). Nor does Pop miss a chance to diss other rising punk superstars of the time, Johnny Rotten from the Sex Pistols in this case, as he reminisces. The interview with Peter Gzowski was on CBC's *90 Minutes Live*. (CBC Digital Archives; https://www.cbc.ca/archives/entry/1977-gzowski-interviews-iggy-pop). An updated CBC archives page at https://www.cbc.ca/archives/the-1977-iggy-pop-tv-performance-that-never-happened-1.5482907 (March 11. 2020) redacted the original 9 minutes.
11. Penman (2022:8).

12 Penman (2022: 8).
13 Ian Penman (2022: 8).
14 Viv Albertine (2014: 208).
15 Cited in van Gijssel (2017).
16 Reddington (2012: 128, 5).
17 See, for instance, McClary (1991, 1992), Moisala and Diamond (2000), Barkin and Hamessley (1999).
18 I discuss in more detail the need to incorporate the tools of musicological analysis for explorations of politics and music elsewhere (Franklin 2005, 2021b).
19 Peraino (2001: 694).
20 See, for example, influential recollections such as *Velvet Goldmine* from Todd Haynes (1998), or *England's Dreaming* from Jon Savage (1991/2001).
21 Stubbs (2018) uses this term as a back-handed insult, or is it compliment, when referring to Throbbing Gristle.
22 Paraphrase and translation of conversation with the artist on April 8, 2023.

Chapter Two

23 Smith (2015: 251).
24 On DIY punk values as an articulation of alternative approaches to the study of world politics see Davies (2005), Dunn (2005, 2016).
25 Two landmark events, which have generated their own dedicated literature, include the concerts under the *Rock Against Racism* mobilization against violent racism and right-wing nationalist parties in the UK, and *Live Aid* in 1985 which heralded the arrival of live, global satellite TV. Punk acts such as the Clash featured prominently in the line-up for the first, and as organizers. Bob Geldof from the Boomtown Rats in particular, in the second.
26 See Reinelt and Rai (2014: 4); Rai et al (2020), Franklin (2021a: 486-90; 2020b). See also Malott and Peña (2004).
27 O'Sullivan (2015: 117-19).
28 Cosey Fanni Tutti (2017: 246-48; 2022: PP).
29 Cosey Fanni Tutti (REF), Black 2011: 41 passim, Smith Start (2016: 119-21) and Albertine ((2015: 378 passim) for their accounts.
30 Black (2011: 46).
31 Black (2011: 406).
32 See Feldstein (2005) and Gaines (2013).
33 Take, for example, Elton John, not punk at all, who elevated these issues to theatrical heights in his 2019 autobiography, *Me*, depicted with all the requisite (queer, camp, boy-child) edginess and boisterousness in the 2019 film adaptation, *Rocketman* (Dir.Dexter Fletcher).
34 UN Women (2022), and World Health Organization (2021).
35 See Frith (2007), Street (2012), and Hesmondalgh (2013) within academic registers. Greil Marcus (1989/2009), Paul Morley (2008), and Jon Savage (1991/2001) provide insider-inflected studies of this period and its underground music-scene. See also Dunn (2005), and Pearson (2021).

36 Reynolds (2022: 21-22).
37 Beaumont-Thomas (2022).
38 This is the call that Reynolds makes (2022: 24).
39 Peraino (2001: 694). See also Peraino, Cusick et al (2013).
40 Joni Mitchell, "Free Man in Paris", from *Court and Spark* (1974).
41 Hynde (2015: xi).
42 In passing, Debbie Harry's band Blondie has become synonymous with Harry herself.
43 I discuss these resonances in Franklin (2021).
44 The daughter of Poly Styrene, the stage name of Marianne Joan Elliott-Said (1957 – 2011), Celeste Bell, has been revisiting her mother's cultural legacy as one of the few punk artists of colour in the formative years of London-based punk in which Poly Styrene's band X-Ray Spex made their mark (Bell and Howe 2019).
45 Gardner (2020: 19-20).
46 See Black 2011: 390 for instance.
47 Hagen (2010). The track was one that former German Chancellor, Angela Merkel, included in her playlist for her retirement party from political office, evoking her East German roots as commentators noted.
48 Hynde (2015: 279).
49 Smith Start (2016: 56, 190-193).
50 Gordon (2015: 173).
51 Tongson (2021).
52 Simone de Beauvoir, her final sentence in the second volume of her memoirs, *The Prime of Life*, (1962: 607).
53 Black (2011: 382).
54 "One is not born, but rather becomes, a woman." (Beauvoir 1949: 267).
55 Peraino citing Elizabeth Freeman (2013; 828, original emphasis).
56 Edgers (2015).
57 Kaitlin Fontana, cited by Hadley Freeman (2016).
58 Freeman (2016).
59 Smith (2016: 253).
60 Nina Simone (1992: ix).
61 Smith (2010: 288).
62 Smith (2015:253).
63 Smith (2015: 275).
64 See Bowers (2002) and Peraino (2001) for feminist takes on these issues.
65 Sheffield (2020).
66 Smith (2022); see also Gaines (2013).
67 Page no. from Hynde.
68 Brownstein (2015: 146, 148, 167-171).
69 Simone (1992: 5).
70 Hynde (2015: 173).
71 Brix Smith Start (2016: 113, 189).

72 Gardner (2020). See also reviews from Fontana (2012) and Freeman (2016).
73 Hynde (2015: 115).
74 Gordon (2016: 273).
75 Smith Start (2016: 182). Part 2 of Start's memoir starts halfway, at page 161-326.
76 Hynde (2015: 234, 235).
77 Small (1998).
78 Hynde (2015: 252).
79 Hynde (2015: 238, 259).

Chapter Three
80 See Petrusich (2019).
81 For the methodologically curious see the Afterword.
82 Alice Bag (b. Alicia Armendariz ,1958) describing how the punk scene took shape on the US West Coast in the late 'seventies, with Los Angeles as the epicenter (2011: 222).
83 Chrissie Hynde (2016: 252).
84 Bag (2011: 183).
85 Reddington (2012) discusses the gender politics of vocal representation.
86 Shaw (2008) discusses this quality to Patti Smith's vocalisations in his study of her first album, *Horses*.
87 Those of Albertine, Hagen, and Hynde who knew him and his girlfriend Nancy Spungen, and also Bag whose reflection is another nuance to this story of drug abuse, intimate partner-violence, and murder (Bag 2011: 237-8).
88 The dilemma, often used in ethics classes, that figures in both studies is about a man facing a difficult decision about how to get crucial medication for his wife who is dying of cancer when he discovers he does not have enough money to pay for the drug. It is called the *Heinz Dilemma* and its various versions are available online: so, how would you, dear reader, respond if in this situation?
89 Gilligan (1983: xv-xxiv).
90 Barthes (1977: 185).
91 Barthes (1987: 183).
92 Barthes (1987: 183.184)
93 To specify; melismatic vocals are on vowels whereas consonants denote syllabic delivery. The latter is very much in play, as sound and rhythm, in the "flow" of the rapping voice in hip hop, and in spoken word delivery.
94 Barthes (1977: 182).
95 See Shaw (2008) on the interventions that Patti Smith made when mixing desk, the (fading in/fading out) vocal tracks in the longer track of *Horses*, "Land".
96 Frith and McRobbie (1978/1990).
97 Pearson (2021: 12).
98 Barthes (1977: 188).
99 Albertine (2014: 206, 221).
100 Albertine (2014: 206).
101 Smith (2010: 179-182).

102 Smith (2010: 182).
103 Smith (2010: 182).
104 Shaw (2008: 48 passim; 68,62). The St Mark's gig is available online, as audio, along with a remix that Smith and Kaye did to commemorate her debut forty years later.
105 Albertine (2014: 79).
106 Bag (2011: 136).
107 Smith (2010: 196). Sam Shepard wrote the play *Cowboy Mouth* (1971) in which he and Patti Smith played the lead roles in the New York production directed by Robert Glaudini.
108 Smith (2010: 186).
109 Phillip Shaw does draw out the vocal delivery that Smith pioneered in his study of Horses....
110 See Shaw (2008: 70).
111 Smith publishes the full poem/lyrics in a compilation of photos, lyrics, and facsimiles at the end of *Just Kids* as an *in Memoriam*, celebrating the life and death of Robert Mapplethorpe (2010: 289 passim).
112 This gig took place in the Markthalle in Hamburg, Germany, broadcast on North German public radio (NDR) on 1 August 1996, released as a bootleg and available online. The playlist featured tracks from her 1996 'comeback' album, *Gone Again*.
113 Hagen (2010: 186-187, Dutch edition, translation my own).
114 See Savage (1991) 2001.
115 Cosey Fanni Tutti (2017: 312).
116 Hagen (2011: 140-41), show also takes a dim view of the recording industry (2011: 181).
117 I discuss "My Way" and Nina Hagen's rendition in Franklin (2020).
118 Bag (2011: 213). She adds, perhaps with the benefit of hindsight; "My face still turns red when I remember it".
119 Hardcore as a next-generation punk sound is the focus of Pearson's study (2021).
120 (Bag 2011: 236).
121 Bag (2011: 212).
122 Smith Start (2016: 236).
123 The playlist was also part of Patti Smith's second set, *Live at the Cellar Door*, Washington DC (Jan 16, 1976); Pumping (My Heart) track 8 in the longer set for that evening.
124 Barthes (2011: 179).
125 Bag encapsulates this tension in a chapter entitled "Coalescence" (2011: 183-84).

Chapter Four

126 Smith (2010: 183-4).
127 Hynde (2016: 213, 217).
128 Hynde (2016: 218, 217). For Hynde on Viv Albertine and the Slits see (2016: 214) and for Albertine on Hynde, see Albertine (2014: 153, 158). See Hynde also on co-writing (2016: 234-235) and the question of punk musicality (2016: 246).
129 Firth and McRobbie (1978/1990).

130 Cosey Fanni Tutti (2017: 243-44).
131 Cosey Fanni Tutti (2022: 122).
132 Pearson (2021: 12-13).
133 Pearson (2021: 13).
134 Pearson's study is premised on these continuities and diversifications (2021: 8 passim). See also Dunn (2016).
135 Pearson (2021: 13).
136 Butler 2006/1990.
137 Albertine (2014: 49).
138 Gordon (2015: 172): "Tunic (Song for Karen)" is on the *Goo* album.
139 See Reddington (2022) and Goldman (2019) on this question.
140 Pearson (2021: 148, emphasis added).
141 See Pearson (2021: 15-17) and Reddington (2012) as two scholar-practitioner-punk fans for how they navigated the academic-practitioner landscape in interviews and fieldwork. Danyel Smith (2022) provides a passionate countermanding account at the intersection of Black women in the music industry, their formative role under-researched.
142 Gordon (2015: 4).
143 Hynde (2015: 190).
144 See Feldman and Hakim (2020).
145 Here she distances herself from McClary to some extent.
146 Albertine (2014: 44).
147 Albertine (2014: 91).
148 Quotes above from Albertine (2014: 91-92).
149 Albertine (2014: 93).
150 Albertine (2014: 104).
151 Albertine (2014: 104).
152 See Connell and Messerschmidt (2005) for a critical review.
153 Albertine (2014: 207, 208; see also 101-4).
154 Albertine (2014: 208).
155 Albertine (2014: 217-8, 221).
156 Albertine (2014: 213-14).
157 Smith Start (2016: 224).
158 Smith Start (2016: 222).
159 Smith Start (2016:224).
160 Smith Start (2016: 182).
161 Smith Start (2016: 225).
162 Gordon (2015; 10).
163 Gordon (2015: 182).
164 Gordon (2015: 203). Danyel Smith (2022) pays attention as well to the unsung influence of the Shangri-Las.
165 Gordon (2015: 203).
166 Gordon (2015: 204).
167 Gordon (2015: 201).

168 Gordon (2015: 204).
169 Gordon (2015: 267).
170 Brownstein (2015: 241)
171 Brownstein (2015: 239-240).
172 Brownstein (2015: 87).
173 Brownstein (2015: 87-88).
174 See Brownstein (2015: 86-88).
175 Brownstein (2015: 62, 182, 183-4, 192).
176 Brownstein (2015: 86, 87).
177 Tweeted from @nowjazznow on 30th September and 23rd October 2022.
178 Albertine (2014: 39).
179 More on this in Franklin (2021).
180 Dunn (2016). See also Davies (2005), Saefullah (2017), Snapes (2015).
181 Barthes (1977: 150).
182 Barthes (1977: 153-4).
183 Barthes (1977: 149), emphasis added.
184 Barthes (1977: 154).
185 Brownstein ((2015: 101, 109, and 110).
186 Hynde (2016: 190).
187 See Pearson (2021).
188 Hynde (2016: 246).
189 Hynde (2016: 234).
190 Gordon (2015: 172), Gordon reprints the letter she wrote "to Karen once, for a magazine, I can't remember which one" in *Girl in a Band* (2015: 173).
191 Gordon (2015: 173). Brix Smith Start writes about her eating disorder issues, and Viv Albertine discusses the effects of cancer treatment on her morphology and body image in the second part of her memoirs.
192 Hynde (2016: 214). Hynde is referring to the American film director and producer, Russ Meyer (1922-2004) who made his name with soft porn films in the mid-twentieth century exploiting sex-gender stereotypes of 'voluptuous' women and *Playboy* inflected nudity. He was briefly associated with Malcolm McLaren's film projects as a vehicle for the Sex Pistols.
193 Koskoff (2000: 2-3).
194 Peraino (2001: 693).
195 See, for instance, Peraino (2001: 694, 2013) and the tripartite framework for feminist approaches to music research in Koskoff (2000: x), Bowers (2002: 11-12, 15) and Diamond (2003), and a colloquy of essays on *Music and Sexuality* curated by Peraino and Cusick (2013).

Chapter Five

196 Black (2011: 406).
197 Channel 4 (dates). Gok Wan became a celebrity with his first show, *How to Look Good Naked*....
198 Smith Start (2016: 435).
199 Hynde (2015: 156).
200 Cosey Fanni Tutti (2017: 148-149).
201 An observation from the audience after a presentation of this work.
202 Cosey Fanni Tutti (2017: 252).
203 Fontana (2012).
204 This is taken from a chapter title (Hynde 2015: 203).
205 Tierney (2019), Hess (2022).
206 Smith (2010: 118-19).
207 Just Kids: 140 (and elsewhere). Shaw (2008: ???).
208 Smith (2010: 232); Smith with Soundwalk Collective (2022).
209 D. Smith (2022).
210 Black (2011: 70, 71).
211 Black (2011: 79, 173-79).
212 Black (2011: 135).
213 Black (2011: 136).
214 Hynde (2016: ??).
215 Hagen (2020: 188-89).
216 Albertine (2014: 223-24) recalls how the photo came about.
217 Hagen (2011: 187, 190-1).
218 Crenshaw (2003); Collins and Bilge (2020).
219 Black (2011: 71).
220 Cosey Fanni Tutti (2017: 413). This is on the issues that a museum in Zurich raised about one of Cosey's exhibitions in 2006 featuring some of the porn magazine work she did years earlier.
221 Cosey Fanni Tutti (2017: 168).
222 Cosey Fanni Tutti (2017: 169).
223 Cosey Fanni Tutti (2017: 171).
224 Black (2011: 160).
225 Black (2011: 183). See also her account of thuggery in audiences, sexism as it intersected with racism while on tour; (2011; 159-163, 180, 194).
226 Cosey Fanni Tutti (2023: 113); Black (2011: 162).
227 For instance, see Albertine (2014: 201), Gordon (2015: 202-203), and multiple statements in Brownstein. Hynde has another take on these matters, and register (2016: 257-8, 278).
228 Hynde (2015: 190).
229 Smith Start page no's.
230 Cosey Fanni Tutti (2017: 340).
231 See Cosey Fanni Tutti (2022: PP).

232	Cosey Fanni Tutti (2017: 171-72).
233	Cosey Fanni Tutti (2017: 171-72).
234	Cosey Fanni Tutti (2022: 125).
235	Pearson (2021: 148 passim).
236	Albertine devotes a chapter to her relationship with Ari Up, barely fifteen at the time (Albertine 2014: 161 passim).
237	Brownstein (2015: 79-224).
238	Brownstein (2015: 109).
239	See Brownstein (2015: 99), Reddington (2007), Coen (2012), and Street Howe (2009).
240	Brownstein (2015: 99, 103, 132, original emphasis).
241	Brownstein (2015: 103-105).
242	Pearson (2021: 148 passim).
243	Cosey Fanni Tutti (2017: 490).
244	Black (2011: 390, 391).
245	Cosey Fanni Tutti (2017: 339, 2022: ???).
246	Cosey Fanni Tutti (2017: 342-43).
247	Bag (2011: 359).
248	See Smith (2010: 64-5, 180-2, 196, 232, 258).
249	She writes fondly about hearing refrains from "Because the Night" from someone's sound system when walking down the street (Smith 2010: 258).
250	Smith (2010: 180-2, 196).
251	Nico was accompanied by alternative, ambient, proto-punk luminaries in the studio such as John Cage and Brian Eno and promoted by agenda-setting DJs of punk and alternative music such as John Peel.
252	Cosey Fanni Tutti (2017: 421-22).
253	Sawyer (2023).
254	Black, in Sawyer (2023). The photo in question is reproduced in the article, it is one that circulates regularly on punk-dedicated social media.
255	As well as publishing her Nicaragua diaries Bag devotes the last chapters of *Violence Girl* to her education about, and with deprived communities in LA and Latin America: Bag (2011: 359-377).
256	Here I am referring to the Annie Lennox album, *Nostalgia*, released in 2014, long after her fame as one of the 1980s New Wave supergroups, the Eurythmics; one of her numerous solo albums.
257	See her chapter, "Kitchen Bitch" (Smith Start 2016: 422) and her approach to competing against Gok Wan on UK television in *Fashion Fix with Gok Wan* (2016: 415, 433).
258	Cosey (2017: 222, 2022: 94-95).
259	Cosey Fanni Tutti (2022).
260	Albertine (2014: 168).
261	See Dunn (2016) and Davies (2005) for considerations of this ethos for the political credibility of punk as a social movement, localised and transnational.

262   Nina Simone (1991: 52).
263   Simone (1991: 159).
264   Brooks (2011: 176). See also Feldstein (2005).
265   Brooks (2011: 180). See also Gaines 2013.
266   Goldman's 2019 memoir-cum-playlist celebrates what she calls the 'She-Punk', with a nod to Kay Weldon's 1983 novel *The Life and Loves of a She-Devil*.
267   See Gaines (2013) and Brooks (2011).

Chapter Six

268   Brownstein (2015: 111).
269   Albertine (2014: 249).
270   Apart from those authors already mentioned, see Molleson (2022), Rogers (2022), D. Smith (2021), Tongson (2021), and Broad (2023).
271   Peraino (2001: 709), see also Reddington (2012).
272   Hynde (2015: 253).
273   Brownstein (2015: 100).
274   Barthes (1977: 149).
275   White (2020).
276   Peraino, (2001: 706).
277   Brownstein (2015: 99). See also Downes (2007, 2012), Marcus (2010), Evans (1997), McDonnell (1997), Raha and Gordon (2004), Bayton (1998), Franklin (2021a).
278   Brownstein (2015: 182, 183).
279   Simone F on DIEM25 (2021); starting at 18 minutes.
280   Caplan (2017).
281   Caplan (2017).
282   Brownstein (2015: 185).
283   Alex Ross has written about this interface for some time (Ross 2010, 2011). See Bleiker (2012) and Shapiro (2004) for takes within the cultural turn in Politics and International Relations departments. For two views on the aesthetics of music see Gracyk (n.d.) and Frith (2009).
284   Barrett (2016: 1).
285   Barrett, citing Mockus (2016: 167).
286   Smith (2010: 59, 165).
287   Beauvoir (1982: 499).
288   Taken from "Another Girl, Another Planet" the single from the Only Ones' 1978 album, *The Only Ones*.